Princess Diana

The House of Windsor

and Palm Beach

AMERICA'S FASCINAT[ION]
"THE TOUCH OF R[OYALTY]"

H. J. ROBERTS, M.D

SUNSHINE SENTINEL PRESS

Library of Congress number TXu 721-401

Includes Index and Photo Section $24.95

Publisher's Cataloging in Publication
           (Prepared by Quality Books Inc.)

Roberts, H. J. (Hyman), 1924-
Princess Diana, The House of Windsor and
Palm Beach: America's fascination with
"the touch of royalty" / H.J. Roberts.
          p. cm.
          ISBN: 1-884243-06-1

1. Palm Beach (Fla.)--History. 2. Visits of state--United States--
1985. 3. Charles, Prince of Wales, 1948 4. Diana, Princess of
Wales, 1961--1. Title.

F319.P2R63 1977   975.9'32
                                             QB196-40796

Photograph of Princess Diana on Front Cover courtesy of
Mort Kaye Studios, Inc., Palm Beach

Printed in the United States of America

Sunshine Sentinel Press, Inc.
P.O. Box 17799
West Palm Beach, FL 33416
FAX (561) 547-8008

Acknowledgements

~

I am grateful to Shirley Brightwell and Kathleen Brightwell for their secretarial services.

Esther Sokol, Stephen Roberts and Jayne Ellison provided valuable suggestions.

The following persons, organizations and companies granted permission to reproduce excerpts and photos, and graciously provided valuable assistance in my researches.

City of West Palm Beach
Davidoff Studios, Palm Beach
The Evening Times
Henry Flagler Museum
Historical Society of Palm Beach County
Journal of the American Medical Association
Lucien Capehart, Palm Beach Photographer
Mort Kaye Studios Inc., Palm Beach
Mrs. Lana Marks
The Miami Herald
News and Sun-Sentinel Company
Norton Gallery of Art
Palm Beach County Department of Airports
Palm Beach Daily News ("The Shiny Sheet")
The Palm Beach Post

Other Books By The Writer

Difficult Diagnosis: A Guide to the Interpretation of Obscure Illness
W. B. Saunders, Philadelphia, 1958

The Causes, Ecology and Prevention of Traffic Accidents
Charles C Thomas, Springfield, 1971

Is Vasectomy Safe? Medical, Public Health and Legal Implications
Sunshine Academic Press, West Palm Beach, 1979

Aspartame (NutraSweet®): Is It Safe?
The Charles Press, Philadelphia, 1990

Sweet'ner Dearest: Bittersweet Vignettes About Aspartame (NutraSweet®)
Sunshine Sentinel Press, West Palm Beach, 1992

Is Vasectomy Worth the Risk? A Physician's Case Against Vasectomania
Sunshine Sentinel Press, West Palm Beach, 1993

A Guide to Personal Peace: The Control of Stress, Depression and Anxiety
(Set of three cassettes) Sunshine Sentinel Press, West Palm Beach, 1993

Mega Vitamin E: Is It Safe?
Sunshine Sentinel Press, West Palm Beach, 1994

West Palm Beach: Centennial Reflections
Sunshine Sentinel Press, West Palm Beach, 1994

The Spirit of Modern Taiwan: Reflections of a Visiting Rotarian
Taipei Southeast Rotary Club, 1994

Defense Against Alzheimer's Disease: A Rational Blueprint for Prevention
Sunshine Sentinel Press, West Palm Beach, 1995

Health and Wealth, Palm Beach Style: Diseases, Behavior and Sexuality of the Rich
Sunshine Sentinel Press, West Palm Beach, 1997

Contents

PREFACE

SECTION I - THE BRITISH ARE COMING

1. Preliminaries 2

2. Great Expectations; Some Royal History 3

3. Invitations 9

4. Controversy 10

5. Coverage by the Media 13

6. Local Critics 15

7. Countering the Critics 18

8. Preparations 20

9. The Envelope 22

SECTION II - EVENTS AT THE NORTON GALLERY OF ART

10. The Norton Gallery Exhibit 25

11. The Norton Gallery Reception/Dinner 27

SECTION III - ROYAL TRIVIA

12. Royal Confessions of a Political Spouse 29

13. A Crash Course on Royal Manners 31

14. More Royal Trivia 35

SECTION IV - THE ARRIVAL

15.   Receiving the Royal Couple 40

16.   Polo Anyone? 43

17.   The Economic Boost 46

SECTION V - THE BALL

18.   Preparations 49

19.   An Ultimate in High Fashion 52

20.   The Dinner/Ball 54

SECTION VI - POSTSCRIPTS

21.   The Instant Celebrities 59

22.   Correspondence 62

23.   More on Polo 64

24.   Armand Hammer (Continued) 66

25.   A Potpourri of Political Fallouts 69

26.   More Postscripts 71

27.   Subsequent Visits by Members of the Royal Family 74

28.   Problems of a Royal Family 81

29.   Di-Vestment by a Fashion Icon 88

SECTION VII - THE DEATH OF PRINCESS DIANA

30.   "The People's Princess": A Tragic Closure 92

31.   Personal Reflections: Overlapping Interests and
      Royal Coincidences 103

32.   Farewells to Diana by Palm Beach 111

PHOTO SECTION .... Center Insert

Glory is a poison, good to be taken in small doses.

— Honoré de Balzac

This is an anachronism of a country so democratic and so informal, yet that still has the latent interest in royalty, pomp and circumstances.

— Bob Graham, United States Senator and
Former Governor of Florida

Preface

A societal bombshell during the Fall of 1985 catapulted Palm Beach onto national and international headlines: the first joint visit of Prince Charles, Duke of Wales, and Princess Diana. The initial five sections describe the various activities that preceded and accompanied this "social event of the Century."

Inasmuch as my wife, Carol, was intimately involved with many of the arrangements in her capacity as Mayor of West Palm Beach, I not only attended each function but also became privy to much related information... some described here for the first time. These personal observations are supplemented by reports and commentaries from reputable news services and other sources. (No collaborators or ghost writers were involved in this effort.)

The reader might ask: "So what?" or "Who cares about these social parasites, especially after their highly publicized separation and divorce?" There are several answers.

First, the activities involving our unique sister-city across the lake have long intrigued Palm Beach-watchers throughout the world -- and continue to do so.

In addition, the ramifications of this visit by the Royal Couple provide extraordinary and oft-sobering insights concerning citizens of the United States. Some of their activities and behavior would have shocked not a few of our founding fathers -- especially awe over "The Touch of Royalty." This fascination seems paradoxic because a middle "class" theoretically should not exist here. In point of fact, most Americans who regard themselves as being "in the middle" usually mean "middle-income."

The ongoing thirst for details about the Princess and Prince, both by the public and historians, further justifies this contemporaneous account. The 12 years of authorship reflect the time often required to evaluate historical and other events accurately, especially as important information and perspectives surface. Examples herein include long-secret insights about Armand Hammer that emerged after the collapse of communist Russia, and the nature of the prolonged discussion between Nigel Marix and the Prince on his arrival.

The difficulties subsequently confronting the Royal Couple and its family appear in Section VI.

Section VII reviews the sudden death of "The People's Princess" at the age of 36 and its worldwide impact. The event precipitated unprecedented mourning by her untold admirers, including many Palm Beachers (Chapter 32). This unforeseen tragic event also brought closure to a personal, albeit brief, acquaintance whose charm, courage and good deeds had profoundly affected me and my work (Chapter 31).

There is no intent of bias, distortion or malice concerning any persons or organizations mentioned.

H. J. Roberts, M.D., F.A.C.P., F.C.C.P.

November 1997

Section I

THE BRITISH ARE COMING

Fame is a food that nourishes and gives us indigestion at the same time.

Sydney J. Harris

1

Preliminaries

West Palm Beach Mayor Carol Roberts found herself involved in many of the plans, tensions, controversies and delights surrounding the forthcoming visit of the Royal Couple on her turf during November 1985.

The Hammer Art Collection

Dr. Armand Hammer, a world-class industrialist (Occidental Petroleum) (Chapter 24), again offered the Norton Gallery of Art in West Palm Beach the opportunity to exhibit his enlarged *Five Centuries of Masterpieces*. The museum immediately accepted because this fabulous collection had proved an enormous crowd pleaser. It confirmed the motto hanging on Hammer's wall: "He who hath the gold maketh the rule."

There was another reason for this gesture. The collection's curator stated: "Dr. Hammer wanted to do something for Prince Charles and Lady Diana." Accordingly, the date of the first showing, November 11, was planned to coincide with the arrival of the Royal Couple on November 12. Rumors circulated that they might visit the museum.

The United World Colleges

Another event was to take place on November 12 -- a fund-raising dinner ball at The Breakers Hotel in Palm Beach.

Most Americans had never heard of the United World College of the American West, the beneficiary of this affair. Dr. Hammer founded the facility in Montezuma, New Mexico as part of a network of United World Colleges in other countries. The Prince of Wales became its nominal head after Lord Mountbatten, his uncle, was killed by a terrorist bomb in 1978.

The United World Colleges were conceived as an nonpolitical vehicle for promoting peace and international understanding through education about the horrors of war. Their students reflect a wide range of social and economic backgrounds; over 95 percent receive some form of financial aid. Lord Mountbatten had been the first President of the Board of Directors. The first college (in Wales) opened its doors during 1962.

2

Great Expectations; Some Royal History

Many regarded this visit of Prince Charles and Princess Diana, however brief, as a social ultimate in the Palm Beach area. It would be the Princess' first trip to the United States.

This "lust for luster" also seemed timely in another respect. It offered a welcome respite from serious world events... including the forthcoming summit meeting between the heads of Russia and the United States. In addition, the visit offered some Americans who had their own "Lady Di" -- in the person of singer Diana Ross -- an opportunity to see the other one.

The significant number of former British residents living in Greater West Palm Beach embellished the occasion. For example, more than 500 persons belonged to the English-Speaking Union of Palm Beach.

There was yet another subtle association between royalty and the wealthy community of Palm Beach. The word "rich" evolved from "Rex"... Latin for king.

The atmosphere became increasingly charged. It was summed in the expression: "The British Are Coming!" Norv Roggen expressed his sentiments in *The Evening Times* (June 4, 1985, p. A-4):

> "I can hardly wait for the royalty season to start. Not the tourist season, but the royalty season, when Palm Beach County rolls out the red carpet for members of the English sovereignty.
>
> "Although we thumbed our noses at those folks in 1776, royalty has never been out of favor in Palm Beach County, and I suspect if we local revolutionaries had a choice today we would willingly become subjects of the king again... Since I don't have a king, maybe I subconsciously admire English royalty...
>
> "Fortunately, there is a place like Palm Beach where the Prince and his beautiful Princess can find the admiration denied them in their own country."[1]

Such excited anticipation, however, was not universal. It seemed a mystery to one *Time* reader that citizens of the United States should be so obsessed with the inconsequential visit of "an effete and parasitic monarchy" (December 2, 1985, p. 5).

James Russell, financial editor of *The Miami Herald*, described this visit and a subsequent one in another light. The headline of his March 6, 1986 (p. D-6) column read: "The British are coming -- to seek investors." A "Britain Means Business" campaign had been launched in Miami seeking American businesses that might consider opening branches in the United Kingdom.

The Historical Paradox

A provision in the U.S. Constitution (Article I, Section 9) prohibits the United States from granting titles of nobility to Americans. It also forbids the acceptance of such titles by persons "holding any office of profit or trust under them" without the consent of Congress. Our Founding Fathers clearly wished to place citizens in the class of "commoners"... permanently.

This situation provided shrewd foreigners who possessed titles the opportunity to dazzle gullible "commoners" with their blue blood. James J. Kilpatrick noted the hunger of the American psyche "to be foreign" (*The Palm Beach Post* November 5, 1995). One columnist joked that the national debt could be decreased significantly by amending this section of the Constitution to enable the offering of titles to the highest bidders.

Persons versed in American history rubbed their eyes in disbelief over the commotion created by this scheduled visit of the Royal Couple. For example, there were lessons on how to address (or not address) royalty, a proper curtsey, and the strict prohibition against wearing tiaras. Someone remarked: "Wasn't this country begun on the premise that its inhabitants didn't want a king of England telling them how to conduct their lives?"

The intrigues involved in getting invited to receptions for the Royal Couple, and the exorbitant prices paid for tickets, also would have confounded the Founding Fathers. A spokesman for the British Embassy in Washington offered this explanation: "Perhaps it's the royalty you gave up" (*The Evening Times* November 8, 1985, p. B-1).

A Florida Pioneer Accepts Royalty

The story of a framer of the first State Constitution of Florida is germane. He planned to assume Scottish royalty until death intervened.

Alexander William Crichton was born on February 6, 1805 at a plantation near the St. Johns River. His devout Presbyterian parents had come from Scotland.

Crichton enlisted in the militia for the Second Seminole War during 1835, and rose to the rank of Major. There was considerable debate among Florida inhabitants thereafter concerning the issue of statehood. Crichton sided with David (Levy) Yulee, champion of this cause. He then became one of the 40 Floridians who signed the document paving the way for admission to the Union.

Crichton later changed careers. He became the ruling elder of the Presbyterian Church in Mandarin... and then in Jacksonville during 1852.

A deceased relative in Scotland left Crichton a large estate. It included a title, a castle, and sufficient money to support the lifestyle of a Scottish nobleman. As Crichton was preparing to move, however, he suffered a "serious stomach trouble" (possibly appendicitis) that proved fatal (*The Miami Herald* March 20, 1995, p. B-3).

The "House of Windsor"

This name for the British royal family dates from July 17, 1917. King George V, a member of the German House of Saxe-Coburg-Gotha -- specifically, Battenberg of Hess -- declared in a proclamation that all descendants of Queen Victoria in the male line who were British subjects would adopt the surname "of Windsor."

A variation occurred following the accession of Queen Elizabeth II in 1952. Her children were to have borne the adopted name of their father... Mountbatten. She declared, however, that the issue of her marriage in the male line would bear the name of either Windsor or Mountbatten-Windsor. Commentators noted that while Mountbatten sounds very British, its origin was as German as sauerkraut.

The Fairy-tale Couple

Much of the American public recalled details of both the courtship and Royal Wedding. It was a natural: the modern-day Prince Charming marrying a beautiful Cinderella with an engaging smile and shy blush. Moreover, she represented the first Englishwoman in 321 years to marry an heir to the throne. Many television viewers placed this Royal Couple on the same wave length as *Dallas* and *Dynasty*... especially "the model Princess" (Chapter 29).

In point of fact, Diana was a member of the Sloane Rangers, the moneyed party-goers who dominate London's upper-class night life. But she had even greater appeal by virtue being one of the world's most photogenic women and also having "the popular Everywoman touch."

Shari Spires explored this "fairy tale" of childhood fantasies (*The Palm Beach Post* November 10, 1985, p. E-1). As the husband of our West Palm Beach Mayor, one passage caught my attention: "Things may have changed in recent years, but when I was a child, a little girl didn't yearn to be president. She dreamed of being a Princess."[2]

Background of the Marriage

The royal family had become increasingly concerned over the apparent preference for bachelor life by 33-year-old Prince Charles. In particular, Earl Mountbatten kept pressing for a suitable marriage in light of the Duke of Windsor fiasco (see below).

A crucial happening occurred after Mountbatten's funeral. Charles was deeply moved by Diana's sincere expression of concern over his overt sadness and loneliness. She had admired Charles as a schoolgirl, displaying a framed photo of the Prince taken at his Investiture in 1969.

Charles proposed to Diana on February 6, 1981 in the nursery at Windsor Castle. (A recent fictional analogy occurred in the movie, *An American President*, when a widowered president began to profess his love in the "Dish Room" of the White House.)

A Déjà Vu

The Duke and Duchess of Windsor

Some longstanding local residents remembered the visits of Edward VIII, another Prince of Wales. Technically the Duke of Windsor on his first visit in 1941, he had abdicated the throne on December 10, 1936 for Wallis Warfield Simpson... "the woman I love." (I still recall my grammar school teacher bringing a radio so that her students could hear these famous words.) He then served as Governor General of the Bahamas.

Volumes have been written about the Duke and Duchess. This section focuses on events in Palm Beach, some not generally known.

The Windsors in Palm Beach

This Royal Couple would return to Palm Beach for one or two weeks during "the season." They usually arrived by train (the way the Duchess wished to travel) -- along with one or two small dogs she called her "children" (Photo Section), her personal maid, the Duke's personal valet, and an enormous amount of luggage.

The couple resided in specially-prepared apartments at the Everglades Club or the Colony Hotel, or at the homes of friends. They included Herbert Pulitzer, Robert Young and former Cuba Ambassador Arthur Gardner. (These *gratis* stays kept one of my friends in the construction business busy remodeling their homes.)

Contrasting with the pair's vilification in Britain (the Queen Mother detested them), they were lionized by Palm Beach's international set as their reigning monarchs. Even Mrs. Post would give a party for the couple.

> We experienced the social electricity generated by the Duke and Duchess of Windsor while dancing in a Palm Beach hotel after dinner. Puzzled by the stares of the audience in our direction, we found them alongside us on the dance floor. Carol was most intrigued by the Duke's unique shoes.

The Duchess reiterated the hope that there wouldn't be "a lot of parties in Palm Beach." It was a foregone conclusion, however, that this would not be the case. The pair had solid bookings from the time they arrived. One social commentator noted that no host would allow them to go "unentertained" in his or her fabulous home. On the other hand, they did respect the Duchess' wish that dinners be kept "intimate" -- meaning not more than 12 guests.

The hosts represented a Who's Who of Palm Beach society. They included the Arthur Gardners, Chris Dunphy, Estee and Joseph Lauder, Bunny and Nicky du Pont, Barton and Walter Gubelmann, Ruth and Joe Tankoos, the Robert Youngs, and the Donahues (of Woolworth fame).

More on the Duke of Windsor

Palm Beachers were familiar with various personal aspects of the Duke. They included his hedonistic early sex life, and probable sterility (attributed to severe mumps as an adolescent). The Duchess allegedly had an affair with Jimmy Donahue, the sadistic Woolworth heir.

The Duke's most detested attitude concerned his pro-Nazi sympathies. Many of the details surfaced in recent years after the British government declassified and released thousands of documents (*The Miami Herald* December 5, 1996, p. A-20). One Foreign Office official remarked that the Duke had "a genius for embarrassment."

- The Duke first met Hitler in 1937.
- Hitler allegedly made him an offer to become the puppet ruler of Britain in the expectation that its war-time government would collapse.

- The Duchess purportedly "desired at any price to be Queen." *The Independent* of London later labeled her "Britain's Would-Be Nazi Queen."
- Winston Churchill was furious over the Duke's behavior. He cabled him on July 1, 1940: "Your Royal Highness has taken active military rank, and refusal to obey direct orders of competent military authority would create a serious situation. I hope it will not be necessary for such orders to be sent. I most strongly urge immediate compliance with wishes of the government."

More on the Duchess

Fascination over the Duchess of Windsor continues to the present. This frumpy woman from poor Maryland beginnings managed to transform herself with stylish elegance, overcame the "empire wrecker" stigma, and attained extraordinary social standing. S. Davies Warfield, her uncle, provided a Florida connection as owner of the Seaboard Airline Railroad that ran from Coleman (Florida) to West Palm Beach.

Marian Fowler gave these insights in *The Way She Looks Tonight*, a biography about five women of style.

- The Duchess had her hair done <u>three times a day</u>!
- She constantly played with her jewels (chiefly from Cartier) as if they were toys.
- Her obsession with jewels was reflected in the fact that charity organizers wishing the Duchess to attend their functions would accompany the invitation with a piece of jewelry.
- She wore understated designer clothes by Schiaparelli, Balenciaga, Dior and Mainbocher.
- Fowler regarded her "34-inch hips" as the Duchess' greatest asset.

Another tribute to her chic and savvy fashion came from cosmetics queen Estee Lauder who hosted anniversary parties for the Royal Couple from 1967 to 1972. Lauder stated, "She always knew what to wear and how to wear it" (*Palm Beach Daily News* April 25, 1986, p. 4).

More on the Jewels

Fascinated by fashion and jewelry, the Duke played an active role in the selection and design of his wife's jewels. He enjoyed buying rare stones, and then working in tandem with jewelers to produce stunning effects. An example is the diamond- and- emerald necklace made by Cartier in 1960. It featured five pear-shaped emeralds (ranging from 5.8 to 14.6 carats) surrounded by diamonds. The Duchess often added a 48.95-carat emerald pendent to the necklace -- also surrounded by diamonds -- once owned by King Alfonso XIII of Spain. This combination was estimated to be worth nearly a half million dollars.

The royal family had a tradition of engraving special sayings on jewelry given by members to each other. The Duke's intimate inscriptions included "My Wallis from her David 19.VI.36," "Hold tight 27-iii-36," and "For our Contract 18-V-37."

Here are other interesting features of "the Windsor fallout."

- The Duchess' jewelry came to be considered both works of art and a solid investment.
- She favored sapphires, apparently believing they brought out the color of her eyes.
- She insisted on having the sleeves of dresses and blouses shortened to avoid covering her bracelets. (Highly conscious of her hands, she tended to keep the fists tight.)
- The Duchess collected a menagerie of animals for jeweled brooches and bracelets, many of which were later copied.

The Duke took pride in these unique jewels. He once expressed the wish that they be dismantled after his wife died so that no one could ever wear them. This hope was not heeded when the jewels were auctioned by Sotheby's in Geneva... the considerable proceeds going to the Institut Pasteur in "appreciation to the people of France."

A Local Apology

There was great embarrassment among members of the Palm Beach County Historical Society when an invited speaker made disparaging remarks about the Royal Couple during their 1961 visit. Circuit Court Judge James R. Knott felt obliged to send this letter on March 31 (courtesy, The Historical Society of Palm Beach County).

H.R.H., The Duke of Windsor, and
The Duchess of Windsor
c/o Honorable Arthur Gardner
830 South Ocean Boulevard
Palm Beach, Florida

Dear Sir and Madam:

As president of the Palm Beach Historical Society, I earnestly hope that you will accept our profound apologies for the remarks of a recent speaker in Palm Beach, who appeared under the auspices of the Historical Society.

Our membership was dismayed and embarrassed by the remarks in question, which came as a complete surprise to all of us. Had we been furnished with an advance copy of the address, we assure you that we would have insisted upon a deletion. We honor and esteem you as distinguished guests who by your presence contribute much to Palm Beach, and at an early date I propose to see to it that an appropriate resolution in that regard is adopted by our organization.

The following response arrived several days later (courtesy, The Historical Society of Palm Beach County).

830 South Ocean Boulevard.
Palm Beach. Florida.

April 2, 1961.

James R. Knott.
Circuit Judge.
County Court House.
West Palm Beach. Fla.

Dear Judge,

The Duchess of Windsor and I thank you very much for your courteous letter of March 31.

The speaker who appeared here recently under the auspices of the Palm Beach Historical Society and to whom you refer, happens, for the last few years, to have been persistently hostile to ourselves.

Although your Historical Society was obviously unaware of this man's phobia, we were not surprized that he took the opportunity here, of indulging once again, in his favorite derogatory topic.

The Duchess and I greatly appreciate your membership's reactions to this speaker's remarks concerning ourselves, and the appropriate resolution in that regard, to be adopted by your organization.

We have pleasure in returning to you, the two pictures of ourselves, duly signed, as requested by your Historical Society.

With our warm regards,

Sincerely Your''s

Edward
Duke of Windsor

Reaction to an Overprotected Duchess

Palm Beachers who had known the Duchess were appalled by the details of her final years. They appear in *The Last Duchess* (Pantheon) by Caroline Blackwood. In her preface, the author provided a startling "lesson" for these friends who were also "vulnerable to being overprotected."

It seems that Maitresse Blum, an octogenarian French attorney, seized control of the Duchess' life after the Duke died from throat cancer in 1972. She was subsequently locked away, literally, in the Paris house given the exiled Windsors by the French government. No one was permitted to visit her. This situation was described by Marchesa Casa Maury as "a horrible old lady being locked up by another horrible old lady" (*Palm Beach Daily News* December 10, 1996, p. 6).

There were rumors that the skin of the Duchess became blackened, and that she shrank to the size of a baby. Even so, *The National Enquirer* (September 14, 1982) reported that this "helpless sleeping beauty" was dressed, coiffed, made up with cosmetics, and fed intravenously... thereby keeping a vow made to the dying Duke about keeping up her looks.

The Duchess died in 1986 at the age of 89. She was buried near the Duke at Windsor Castle's Frogmore Garden Cemetery.

An Extraordinary Coincidence

A remarkable set of circumstances would later interweave the timing of a planned sale of the estate of the Duke and Duchess of Windsor with mourning over the untimely death of Princess Diana (Chapter 30). Sotheby's announced that this auction of more than 40,000 objects from their "petit palace" at 34 Route de Champs Entraiment in Paris, many with royal ciphers, would occur during September 1997.

> Among the mementos of this great love story was the 1755 George III mahogany "Abdication Desk." After reigning for less than a year, King Edward VIII signed the Instrument of Abdication on it at 10:30 AM on December 10, 1936 so that he could marry the previously twice-married Wallis Simpson. Parliament accepted it the next day.

There was yet another coincidence: Mohamed al-Fayed, Diana's possible future father-in-law, owned the estate. A commentator for *The Wall Street Journal* wondered how much money would be generated by "a man whose contribution to history was running away from it" (August 18, 1997, p. A-13).

Another Déjà Vu

I recalled another event during 1980 that involved Prince Charles. He experienced heat exhaustion while playing polo, and then landed in a room at the Good Samaritan Hospital adjacent to the one occupied by a patient of mine (Chapter 12).

[1]©1985 *The Evening Times*. Reproduced with permission.
[2]©1985 *The Palm Beach Post*. Reproduced with permission.

3

Invitations

"*Guess Who's Coming To Dinner?*"

This pertinent caption appeared on the October 28, 1985 cover of *Newsweek*. It recalled the movie hit in which a young white socialite brought a black fiance to dinner without her parents being aware of his race.

Many well-known personalities would be coming to the dinner/ball as benefactors or entertainers... without any guess work. They included Bob Hope, Victor Borge, Gregory Peck, Cary Grant, Merv Griffin, Malcolm Forbes, Ted Turner, "Dear Abby," H. Ross Perot, Louis Nizer and Joan Collins.

Social One-upmanship

Several dozen local notables, chiefly residents of Palm Beach, planned to attend The Ball after purchasing tickets at $5,000 each. Most anticipated the event with glee. Some even produced their own contemporaneous royal-type receptions. One selected "D-Day minus 2" (the Sunday before arrival of the R.C.) to entertain some of the arriving visitors... using the facility of a wealthier friend to enhance her social status.

The Palm Beachers planning to attend generally took this happening in stride. A few joked about the invitation. Lewis Widener stated: "I'm very disappointed the invitation was so simple. I expected gold tassels and crowns" (*News/Sun-Sentinel* October 20, 1985, p. A-17).

The Scramble for Tickets

This dinner/dance affair in the offing gave new meaning to the word "exclusive." Nationwide, "household name" personalities exerted pressure for access to a perceived societal ultimate. Their zeal for obtaining tickets intensified when Buckingham Palace told Washington that the Royal Couple did not wish to see "the same faces" at every event.

A mad scramble ensued for invitations to meet the Royal Couple -- both during their preceding D.C. visit and in our area. Persons having political and economic clout expected this "favor" from their connections at the White House and in Congress... the national centers of obligatory "perquisities" (perks).

- The wife of one prominent tycoon allegedly uttered, "I'll kill," if she did not get invited (*The Palm Beach Post* October 13, 1985, p. A-6).
- Some socialites and business executives utilized another approach: exploiting their family or corporate ties to Britain.
- *Time* (November 11, 1985, p. 56) referred to the "select Seraphim of the monied and powerful" who would be meeting the Royal Couple during their visits to Washington and Palm Beach.

Senator Paula Hawkins of Florida clued us to the popularity of the Royal Couple at a small dinner gathering. She mentioned the steady stream of requests over the years from bigwigs seeking an audience with the Prince and Princess. No others even came close. Hawkins' experiences were duplicated by her colleagues, who kept pleading with the White House to repay the political favors of major supporters.

4

Controversy

Announcement of the visit by the Royal Couple generated intense controversy in our sister-city. Indeed, it could be equated to an "8" on the social Richter scale. As author of a history on the Greater West Palm Beach area, WEST PALM BEACH: CENTENNIAL REFLECTIONS (Sunshine Sentinel Press, 1994), I could not recall a previous or subsequent event that had precipitated so much sustained social and political debate.

"The Night Of Stars" on Saturday, November 18, 1992 celebrated the grand opening of the Raymond F. Kravis Center for the Performing Arts in West Palm Beach. This occasion culminated years of philanthropy and planning aimed at providing the community with a world-class auditorium and stage. But many considered the price for attending this social and cultural spectacle -- $1,000 per person -- "outrageous."

Ticket Prices

Old-time Palm Beachers regarded the price of $5,000 per ticket to attend the dinner/ball as obscene. Little wonder. The costliest tickets for a "royal" function during the previous season went for $500 each. This dinner party by the Preservation Foundation of Palm Beach at Mar-a-Lago (the 118-room seaside mansion of the late Marjorie Merriweather Post) featured Thailand's Queen Sirikit.

Town Council President Paul Ilyinsky, himself the son of a Russian Grand Duke, exclaimed: "Ten thousand dollars! What are they going to serve, duck stuffed with gold?"

Foreign Beneficiaries

Many residents expressed concern that the monies raised were going out of the country. E.T. Smith, a former Ambassador to Cuba and Mayor of Palm Beach, asserted: "I think it takes a hell of gall for someone to come in here and collect money for a foreign nation" (*The Miami Herald* September 18, 1985, p. PB-11).

Taxpayer Costs

There was a dither over the required security -- or more to the point, the estimated high cost of providing adequate police protection and surveillance. Nancy Douthit, a member of the Town Council, bemoaned the projected expense. *The Miami Herald* (November 10, 1985, p. A-14) quoted her: "Diana can't even go to the ladies' room without someone rushing in to see if there's a bomb in the tank."

Excluded Locals

About fifty Palm Beachers were invited. The excluded others vented their indignation and frustration... most often obliquely. They attacked "the very nerve" of mailing invitations before the Town Council had officially approved this event on its turf -- an objection based on one of the Town's remarkable ordinances.

Council President Ilyinsky claimed that "about 95% of the people I've talked to are against having the ball" (*The Miami Herald* September 18, 1985, p. PB-1). But he nevertheless asked Alan Cummings, another member of the Council: "How come you're the only one of the Council that got an invitation?" (*The Miami Herald* September 20, 1985, p. C-1).

A headline in the October 4 edition of the *Palm Beach Daily News* poured acid onto the perceived social snub concerning "tickets to royal favor." It read: "THE INVITATION: Did You Get Yours? If So, You're One in 50."

The society editor began: "Those who haven't yet received one daren't ask who has." She suggested that persons in this category should begin making travel plans in order to be "conspicuously out of town" on the night of November 12. One hint: visit a long-lost cousin being married in Bali the same night.

This editor offered another suggestion to those who had received an invitation, but were not going: "Carry yours around in your pocket or purse. That way when you casually drop the fact, you can offer proof" (*Palm Beach Daily News* November 8, 1985, p. 1).

A "Bought" Permit?

A feature in the September 19 edition of *The Miami Herald*   (p. PB-1) suggested a payoff. It began: "When it comes to royalty, even the Town of Palm Beach can be bought." The Council had voted 4-1 to approve The Ball -- but only after the planners offered $75,000 to its Community Chest. The *Palm Beach Daily News* (p. 3) published the Town's Permission for Charitable Solicitation Permit No. 241-86 on September 25, 1985.

Council President Ilyinsky was now on the spot. Joking about feeling like a "highwayman," he acknowledged that it "may have looked like moral blackmail, but there's a very thin line between legality and morality" (*The Palm Beach Post* October 7, 1985, p. A-4).

Former Ambassador E. T. Smith, also serving on the Preservation Foundation of Palm Beach, lashed out at this token donation (*The Miami Herald* October 6, 1985, p. E-2). He argued that $75,000 represented only 3.75 percent of the anticipated funds raised. Smith also pointed out that the remainder would go to a college in New Mexico having only two students from Florida.

Montezuma's Revenge

Attacks were leveled at the United World College of the American West in Montezuma, referred to as a "transitional institution" -- that is, between high school and college. The international baccalaureate degree received by students on completion would be counted as a freshman year only in those colleges and universities accepting such credits.

Some criticized one of the school's service programs, "Wilderness Service and Survival." It included mountain rescue experiences.

Writing the *Palm Beach Daily News* (October 13, 1985, p. A-9) about this college, a reader asked, "Do we really need Montezuma's revenge?"

Subsequent biographers of Hammer shed light on his motivation for this project -- namely, a quest for the Nobel Peace Prize (Chapter 24).

More on Dr. Hammer

Dr. Armand Hammer received much Red flak from a cadre of blue-blooded Palm Beachers. They regarded this certified friend of Lenin as a closet Communist... suspicion reinforced when classified Soviet documents became available after the collapse of communism (Chapter 24). Others wondered in public whether his college was "a training ground for the KGB" (*The Miami Herald* October 5, 1985, p. PB-1). As further evidence of the "Soviet Connection," they noted that Hammer had brought his personal physician to see the late Soviet Premier Konstantin Chernenko.

Hammer graduated from Columbia University College of Physicians and Surgeons in 1921. He visited Bolshevik Russia while waiting to start a coveted internship at Bellevue Hospital in New York City. (Subsequent biographers suggested that this drastic change of plans occurred because Armand had botched a fatal abortion for which his doctor-father took the rap.) Hammer's ties to the country became solidified by (a) marrying a Russian Baronessturned-entertainer, (b) operating factories there, and (c) becoming the sole American concessionaire for the Ford Motor Company and U.S. Rubber.

Palm Beachers received plain envelopes that contained derogatory material about "the poor Red Billionaire, Dr. Armand Hammer." An unsigned pamphlet referred to him as "the Kremlin connection." It emphasized his father's role in forming the American Communist Party during 1919. Hammer's Jewish roots also gave bigots more ammunition.

Reporting on this "sneak attack," *The Miami Herald* (October 4, 1985, p. E-1) noted that one brochure came from the Liberty Lobby, which it described as a "pressure group for patriotism." Council President Ilyinsky told the press that he lined his three parrot cages with copies of this anonymous pamphlet. Ilyinsky asserted: "If they don't have the decency to sign it, then to hell with them" (*The Palm Beach Post* October 7, 1985, p. A-4).

There were assertions that Hammer's wealth and business connections had financed Soviet espionage in the United States, a belief pursued by J. Edgar Hoover... and ultimately documented.

One career anti-Communist, determined to prevent the forthcoming Palm Beach visit, referred to Hammer as "an agent of the Kremlin" (*The Palm Beach Post* October 15, 1985, p. B-1). He further alleged that the purpose of the United World Colleges was to "train students to become the bureaucracy of an already planned Marxist-minded-and-structured world government, to which the United States is expected to surrender its sovereignty, a cause to which Hammer is warmly dedicated."

Some officials of B'nai B'rith's Anti-Defamation League referred to this 86-year-old man as "an expert in anti-Semitic innuendo."

Others resurrected Dr. Hammer's conviction nine years previously for having made an illegal contribution of $100,000 to the 1972 presidential campaign of Richard Nixon. (It may have represented most of the funding of the Watergate cover-up.) The judge took pity on the then-77-year-old man sitting in a wheelchair, constantly monitored by his physician. Hammer was fined only $3,000 and placed on a one-year probation after pleading guilty to misdemeanor charges. President George Bush later pardoned this wrist-slap conviction. *The Palm Beach Post* (November 10, 1985, p. F-1) reflected that the tycoon showed "no signs of imminent demise" during his Palm Beach visit.

5

Coverage By The Media

The print and electronic news media had field days galore while reporting on, or joking about, the visit of the Royal Couple.

"The Shiny Sheet"

On October 30, 1985, the *Palm Beach Daily News* began a series about "The Royal Visit" notwithstanding negative feelings by some of its subscribers (Chapter 4). The first installment carried the subtitle, "D-Day Minus 13." The numbers then decreased as D-Day neared. Considering the increased newsstand sales, even those who pooh-poohed the event probably read every detail when no one was looking.

Alex S. Jones, a reporter for *The New York Times*, recalled that many sophisticates had denounced the Royal Wedding, but managed to get up at 3 AM to watch the entire event on television (*The Miami Herald* November 11, 1985, p. A-10).

"Lost" Invitations

A D-Day editorial in *The Palm Beach Post* (November 12, 1985, p. A-12) sought to soothe the disappointment of those still expecting invitations under the caption "What! No Invitation?" It began: "U.S. Postal Service must do the decent thing, and accept the blame for losing all those invitations that didn't arrive for the big events surrounding today's Royal Visit."

Florida Representative James Thompson told the *Palm Beach Daily News* that his invitation may have been lost in the mails. He added: "I'm a country boy. They probably wouldn't want me there" (November 9, 1985, p. 1).

Local Jokesters

This visit by the Royal Couple tickled the funny bone of regional reporters and talk-show hosts. (Also see Chapter 6.)

Charity In Reverse

Members of the local media expressed pity for Palm Beach because the funds raised there were destined to leave "Town." Ron Wiggins, a feature writer for *The Palm Beach Post*, suggested a "sock hop" to help find a cure for Grundy's disease (November 17, 1985, p. C-1). (He defined this condition as "a hysterical disorder suffered by the Delicately Constituted.") Funds were to be raised <u>outside</u> Palm Beach, and brought here for this -- or any other -- good cause. Wiggins concluded with this variation of a famous ethnic educational promo: "A town is a terrible thing to waste."

Seeking Information

Rick Ackermann, a writer for *The Palm Beach Post*, fantasized about questions the Royal Couple might be asked (October 12, 1985, p. C-1). His imagination included this one for Mayor Carol Roberts, surrounded by Queen of

Hearts Escorts: "Ask them why don't they get rid of Pindling" (Prime Minister of the Bahamas)?

Digs By Dave Barry

Remarks in a column by Dave Barry titled, "The Royal Beat" (*The Miami Herald* November 11, 1985, p. A-10), provoked some readers.

- "The correct form of address for Charles is to say: 'Your Wacking Great Humongous Worshipfulnees, May I Lick The Bacteria Off Your Instep?'"
- "As for Diana, you address her as: `You Stuck Up Little Twit.'"

Barry also conjectured that Diana had been recruited "in a desperate attempt to improve the Royal Gene Pool."[1]

National Jokesters

"Royal" puns and pseudo-puns began to permeate the land. Some examples are mentioned.

The Diet Thing

One observer envisioned the first conversation between Nancy Reagan and Princess Diana on National Public Radio. She inferred a major topic of mutual interest: remaining thin without giving a hint of dieting. It had the ring of an adage familiar in Palm Beach circles: "You can't be too rich or too thin."

Art Buchwald's Two Cents

Art Buchwald was pleased to report that while most others in the nation's Capitol were "behaving like idiots trying to wangle an invitation to one of the glittery affairs," he and his wife couldn't care less (*The Palm Beach Post* October 22, 1985, p. A-14). Inasmuch as Ms. Manners had written that one is not supposed to talk to the Royal Couple unless first spoken to (see below), Art failed to see why getting invited was such a big deal.

Digs At Palm Beach

Palm Beach and its inhabitants came under merciless scrutiny by the international press.

- *The New York Times* quipped that Palm Beach gossip "can be 24-karat" because of the wealth, power and other attributes of its residents.
- *The Miami Herald* quoted one reporter: "These old biddies have only one thing tighter than their egos, and that is their facelifts" (November 14, 1985, p. A-12.)

[1]©1985 *The Miami Herald*. Reproduced with permission.

6

Local Critics

The public relished many morsels about the modus operandi of "high society" in Palm Beach as accounts concerning the antics of its "loyal minority" surfaced.

A Royal Pain in the Neck

Some old-time Palm Beachers gave the forthcoming events a cool reception and collective ho-hum. These dissidents regarded the incursion by Dr. Hammer and the Royal Couple as a "royal pain in the neck." Some reactions:

- The *Palm Beach Daily News* called an annoyed Mrs. James Akston about The Ball being held the next day. Her answer was to the point: "I have nothing to say about that party."
- William E. Hutton III stated: "I think it's terrific that they're coming... But really, we get royalty all the time" (*The Miami Herald* November 10, 1985, p. A-14).
- Vincent Draddy, a former chairman of the Izod Corporation, told the *Palm Beach Daily News* (November 13, 1985, p. 2): "I think it takes a hell of a nerve by Hammer... most Palm Beach people I know aren't going to the party."

Ken Cruickshank of *The Evening Times* opined about the dismay of some Palm Beachers over this touted premiere social event of the season (November 8, 1985, p. B-1).

> "Palm Beach isn't what it use to be... After all, Prince Charles and Lady Di aren't going to Palm Springs or Newport; they're coming to Palm Beach -- and this is disturbing the even tenor of the lives of those who have been presiding over the old town's slow slide into social oblivion for so long that they've never noticed it hasn't really happened. They're upset because they're having their noses rubbed in the fact that Palm Beach may still be pretty chic after all. They're not quite sure they like the idea... the truth is that they aren't what they use to be and aren't, basically, interested in turning back the clock."[1]

Such inappropriate hostility occasionally generated humor. One well-known resident retracted her angry comment after realizing that the visitor was the Prince of Wales -- not the rock star Prince (*The Miami Herald* November 18, 1985, p. C-1).

Guess Who's Not Coming To Dinner?

David Marcus of *The Miami Herald* noted: "Everybody, just everybody, won't be there" (October 27, 1985, p. A-1). Similarly, a columnist for the *Palm Beach Social Pictorial* observed: "I haven't heard of a soul, not a soul, who's going. It's very curious" (*The Miami Herald* October 27, 1985, p. A-16).

Governor and Mrs. Bob Graham planned to greet the Royal Couple at Palm Beach International Airport on their arrival, but would not be attending The Ball.

Some respected Palm Beachers were invited, but declined to attend in person. The Kenan family (Flagler Systems) was represented by Nadine House. She described them as "very unpretentious people (who) wouldn't do anything like this" (*Palm Beach Daily News* November 11, 1985, p. 6).

Societal Revenge... Palm Beach Style

Residents of Palm Beach and its environs fought back at the Hammer "invasion" in their unique ways. A number of socialites specifically indicated that they planned NOT to attend "The Ball."

- Gregg Dodge, widow of the auto tycoon, explained: "That's the day I have my legs waxed."
- Purportedly having thrown out her invitation, Mollie Wilmot (famed for her three rich husbands and the rusted ship, the Mercedes, that once nestled in her backyard) stated: "I'd rather give more to a charity I care about than feed a man's ego trip."
- Helene Tuchbreiter had no reluctance informing national television that she hadn't been invited to The Ball. She also relayed this dinner comment of a friend: "It's Di this, Di that. If I hear anymore about her, I think I'll die" (*The Miami Herald* October 27, 1985, p. A-16).
- Roxanne Pulitzer described the visit as "a media blitz" (*The Miami Herald* November 11, 1985, p. A-1), but apparently had not been invited.

Here are more variations on this theme.

A. Palm Beach has its special vocabulary of social venom. One hostess gleefully quipped: "I think they'll have to paper the room." (This severe disgrace on the charity scene refers to packing an event with non-paying guests.)

B. The concomitant exhibition of *Five Centuries of Masterpieces* intensified the rage of some "regulars" in Palm Beach's charity circuit. One socialite complained that Armand Hammer was "trying to run a one-man show in town" (*The Miami Herald* October 27, 1985, p. A-16).

C. These gala events in both Washington and Palm Beach generated jokes about not having been invited. The invitation to Sergeant Shriver's 70th birthday on November 9 read: "If you're not involved with Royalty, come celebrate my birthday instead" (*Newsweek* October 20, 1985, p. 71).

D. An exclusive non-royal party took place the same night as The Ball on Manalapan, an affluent community to the south of Palm Beach. Invitations reading "Without the presence of Their Royal Highnesses" were sent to only 20 persons. They paid $4,995 a person -- $5 cheaper than the gala event being held at The Breakers. Whereas only the Princess of Wales was permitted to wear a tiara at The Ball, female guests attending this function HAD to wear tiaras and crowns.

E. The aforementioned Helene Tuchbreiter told the *Palm Beach Daily News* (November 14, 1985, p. A-10) of her plans for that evening: sitting in a nice warm tub with Epsom salts.

F. Mary Woolworth Donahue had a few friends over for dinner. She commented: "The Duke and Duchess of Windsor used to come and visit me and my husband all the time. I've seen so much of this all my life, so why should I go and take up space when some young person could go who's never seen any of this?" (*Palm Beach Daily News* November 14, 1985, p. A-10).[2]

E.R. Bradley's Saloon featured a "Charles and Diana Look-Alike Contest" that evening. The establishment rolled out a royal red carpet for the occasion. Unfortunately, no one resembling either the Prince or the Princess showed up.

The Palm Beach Grande Dame

Mary Sanford, referred to by *Town & Country* Magazine as the Queen of Palm Beach, had succeeded Marjorie Merriweather Post... also described as "The American Empress." Sanford initially planned to attend The Ball, but then had second thoughts. She qualified having accepted its <u>chairmanship</u> with the statement: "I wouldn't do it again. I sort of resent this man (Hammer) coming in. He's not my type. I think the money raised in Palm Beach ought to stay in the community" (*The Miami Herald* October 27, 1985, p. A-16).

Sanford then made it clear that a lot of her friends also did not like Dr. Hammer. She felt that Hammer "just keeps appointing, and it confuses everything. I don't think he knows very much about doing this kind of thing." But she added: "He has a lot of courage to come here" (*The Miami Herald* November 3, 1985, p. A-24).

Palm Beach's chief organizer continued anguishing over her misconception that The Ball was to be held in honor of the Royal Couple... not Dr. Hammer. Had she known, this Grande Dame "would have thought twice about doing it... I don't usually associate with that kind of people" (*The Palm Beach Post* November 12, 1985, p. A-12).

Push came to shove when Mary Sanford boycotted the affair. Her social secretary notified the United World Colleges on November 10 -- "D-Day minus two" -- that the chairperson of The Ball would be "unable to attend" (*Palm Beach Daily News* November 10, 19085, p. A-1). Graciously, she didn't seek a refund of the $5,000 for her ticket.

It was conjectured that Sanford's personal calls about her decision influenced others in the elite ranks of Palm Beach society to send their regrets (*Palm Beach Daily News* November 12, 1985, p. A-4).

Pat Kluge

Some innocents were caught in this web of nitpicking and maneuvering among Palm Beach's "high society." A case in point was the downgrading of Pat Kluge, wife of billionaire John Kluge, as general chairman of The Ball. Word got out that she had been asked to resign (*Palm Beach Daily News* November 1, 1985, p. 1).

To those who knew Pat Kluge (Chapter 7), this snub seemed hypocrisy at its worst. Part of the problem centered around her having been photographed in the 1970s for the British magazine *Knave* as a full frontal nude.

The Kluges indicated they would be traveling abroad on D-Day.

7

Countering The Critics

Many residents of the Greater West Palm Beach area decried the discourtesy being exhibited to the Royal Couple and Dr. Hammer by some Palm Beach denizens.

- The Reverend John Mangrum of St. David's Episcopal Church in Wellington took off his holy gloves. The "Polo Priest" stated that he was "disgusted with the maudlin cries of wounded anguish coming from Palm Beach ...They should bring the ball and the dinner over here to the Polo Club and leave Palm Beach out of it (*The Town-Crier* November 21, 1985, p. A-2). He told *The Evening Times*: "The rudeness Palm Beach has shown to Hammer and the Prince and Princess is symptomatic of the insecurity most nickel millionaires have in themselves... We welcome them" (October 21, 1985, p. C-1).
- Governor Bob Graham of Florida also got into the act by declaring November 12 as Armand Hammer Day in the State.

Palm Beach Anglophiles

The Anglophiles of Palm Beach got in their licks. Celia Lipton Farris, a prominent socialite raised in England, planned to attend The Ball with her daughter. She decried the critics. "I wish they'd stop all the gossip and leave well enough alone. I feel very badly that we have all this going on. Let's show some respect... Perhaps the next time they come, they'll get lucky -- and a few people like myself can run it" (*Palm Beach Daily News* November 4, 1985, p. 1).

Criticism of the decision by the Royal Couple to stay in their own Wellington home, rather than on Palm Beach, disturbed others. Ian R. B. Nairnsey, a Brit living in Wellington, commented on their preference for out-of-town life (*The Miami Herald* October 27, 1985, p. E-2): "To refer to the Polo and Country Club as *nouveau riche* shows ignorance both of the area and of the French language."

Many other Anglophiles now living in Palm Beach welcomed the visit with memories of British pomp and circumstance.

Ann Anderson and her mother watched the coronation of Queen Elizabeth II. She still has the chair and stool on which they observed the event (*Palm Beach Daily News* June 19, 1997, p. 1) The royal insignia "ER II" is embroidered in gold on front. Anderson was one of the last young women from the United States to be presented at court. The godfather of her English-born maternal grandmother was the first Duke of Wellington.

The Press

Local editors were aghast at the criticism being leveled at Hammer. *The Palm Beach Post* editorialized on October 17 (p. A-20):

"Armand Hammer's charities are his own business, as is his friendship with British royalty and Soviet bureaucrats. If Palm Beach residents want to pay a king's ransom to dance with the Prince and Princess, that's up to them.

"But let the public not forget that in 1980-1981, Hammer brought to the Norton Gallery his Five Centuries collection, the finest art exhibit (held) in that institution. In 1982 he loaned the Norton his magnificent Honore Daumier collection, another popular success. This year he is bringing an expanded Five Centuries collection that promises to eclipse anything the gallery has ever known.

"It would be a shame if his visits here, and his contributions to this community, were marred by irresponsible name calling and mindless gossip."[1]

The Miami Herald captioned its front-page feature on November 3, 1985: "Worldy Tycoon Getting Icy Palm Beach Welcome." It stated: "Perhaps never before has such a powerful figure been given such a shabby welcome. In fact, the 87-year-old oil tycoon may be the only capitalist in the world who get friendlier treatment in Moscow than in Palm Beach."

George McEvoy, a feature writer for *The Evening Times*, wrote this letter (November 4, 1985, p. A-4) to express his apologies, and extended a personal invitation to the Royal Couple.

"Dear Charles and Di,

"Well, they've certainly made a mess out of your visit to the colonies, haven't they?... I'm extending this invitation to you because it's really crummy the way they're treating you over in Palm Beach, and we don't want you to go back to the castle and tell dear old mummy how loutish the colonists were to you."[2]

Some societal commentators on the national scene also were turned off by the maneuvering involved in these "disgusting spectacles."

Pat Kluge (Continued)

Pat Kluge allegedly had been asked to resign as general chairman of The Ball to avoid a Royal Blush because some London papers were sensationalizing the revelation that she had posed nude for a sex magazine (Chapter 6). After marrying John Kluge, she earnestly involved herself with many charitable causes.

Mayor Carol Roberts regarded these ongoings as hypocrisy. She confided: "After all, no one seemed to object when Greg Dodge raised money for Girls Town. But it was that project, and the way in which the monies were handled, that forced the Town of Palm Beach to pass its present ordinances regulating fund-raising."

Letters to the editor reinforced this inappropriate resurrection of Kluge's past. Bernadette Nestor wrote *The Evening Times* (November 13, 1985, p. A-4):

"I am sending this letter to voice my opinion on the disassociation of Mrs. John Kluge from the fund raiser ball in honor of the royal couple.

"Last year I attended another fund raiser in honor of Mr. Kluge in New York City. I had the distinct pleasure of being in the presence of Mr. and Mrs. Kluge. I and many others observed the tasteful and elegant manner in which Mrs. Kluge performed that evening.

"The patrons at the ball in Palm Beach will be the losers, not having the opportunity to be in the company of this beautiful, charming and graceful woman. Would anyone dare resurrect the past of Prince Charles and Lady Diana and their families? Heavens! The ball might have to be canceled.

"I am not surprised at the hypocrisy, insensitiveness and shortsightedness of the ball organizers. Out here in reality land, people have the ability to see the ocean for the breakers.[3]

[1] ©1985 *The Palm Beach Post*. Reproduced with permission.
[2] ©1985 *The Evening Times*. Reproduced with permission.
[3] ©1985 *The Evening Times*. Reproduced with permission.

8
Preparations

Local history buffs couldn't recall another event in the Palm Beaches -- including the stays of President John F. Kennedy -- that had stimulated as much excitement, activity and planning.

Flowers

Janet Hooker, sister of publisher Walter Annenberg, footed the bill for flowers at The Ball. They included many from her own greenhouse, and more than 3,000 bunches of orange- and peach-colored tiger lilies and bittersweet freesias that were being flown in from Holland.

Limousines

Nearly every black, blue and silver limousine in Palm Beach, Broward and Dade Counties -- about 50 -- was committed to shuttle the Royal Couple and dozens of other "out-of-town" visitors to the polo game in distant Wellington on November 12. (But there were to be no white limousines.) All the chauffeurs required complete security clearances.

The cost of leasing these limos ranged from $400 to $500 a day, plus the customary 15% gratuity for drivers (*The Miami Herald* October 27, 1985, p. A-16).

Personal Diplomacy

Speculation mounted in mid-September that this fund-raiser ball would be cancelled or held elsewhere. Why? It seemed likely that the Palm Beach Town Council would vote against having it held on its premises! The world read about such only-in-Palm-Beach *chutzpah* with disbelief.

> A writer for *The Evening Times* (September 18, 1985, p. B-2) fancied that the Council might find itself in the same role as Oliver Cromwell. He had booted King Charles I off the throne in 1683 over a money dispute, and later beheaded him. Two facts were not overlooked by some history mavens: (1) the current Prince had the same name as Charles I and Charlemagne (Charles the Great); and (2) Mayor Yvelyne de Marcellus ("Deedy") Marix of Palm Beach claimed to be a direct lineal descendant of Charlemagne.

At that point, Mayor Carol Roberts held a crucial meeting with several British representatives. "Her Honor To The West" expressed enthusiastic willingness to host the event in West Palm Beach. She also suggested an acceptable alternate location: the soon-to-be-opened prestigious Governor's Club at Phillips Point. Its executives could not restrain their delight at the prospect.

Roberts was asked two questions: "Would West Palm Beach offer police security?", and "How much would West Palm Beach charge for such protection?" She immediately replied with a "Yes" to the first question, and "Nothing" to the second.

The planners breathed a sigh of relief, reassured about having a contingency red carpet for the Royal Couple. Although Carol was not made privy to the details of ensuing negotiations, she suspected that her personal intervention had an impact when the Town Council approved The Ball that very night!

Presenting The Key

Another difficulty arose over the key-to-the-city issue because the Town of Palm Beach doesn't have such a "key." Once again, Mayor Roberts came to the rescue by arranging for a key, which she was requested to present. Michael Hewitt, Her Majesty's Consul, would transmit the memento to the Royal Couple. Carol explained to the press: "They asked me if I would mind giving it to the British Consul to forestall any diplomatic repercussions" (*The Evening Times* October 21, 1985, p. C-1).

This ceremony took place at The Breakers Hotel one day before the Prince and Princess arrived (see Photo Section).

9

The Envelope

Monday evening, October 1. Mayor Carol Roberts returned late because several conferences followed the City Commission meeting. She then pulled a large envelope from her briefcase addressed to Mayor Carol Roberts and Dr. H. J. Roberts. It had been postmarked in Los Angeles on September 26, 1985. Handing it to me, Carol teased: "Oh, Love, you might be interested in something that came in my mail."

I found three invitations. The **first** was from the Board of Directors of the Armand Hammer United World College of the American West. It requested the pleasure of our company to The Ball "in the presence of Their Royal Highnesses, the Prince and Princess of Wales." The actual invitation is reproduced.

In the Presence of Their Royal Highnesses
The Prince and Princess of Wales
The Board of Directors
of
The Armand Hammer United World College
of the American West
Requests the Pleasure of Your Company
at a Gala in Honor of
Dr. Armand Hammer
for his contributions to
The International Movement of
the United World Colleges

Tuesday, the Twelfth of November
Palm Beach, Florida

7:30 p.m. Reception   The Breakers
8:45 p.m. Dinner   Palm Beach, Florida
Black Tie
R.S.V.P. by October 15, 1985

In view of the prior discussion (Chapters 6 and 7), readers might find the accompanying list of chairpersons and members of the Board of Directors of interest.

General Chairmen

Mr. and Mrs. John W. Kluge   Mr. and Mrs. Jerry Weintraub

National Co-Chairmen

Mrs. Milton Petrie   Mr. Alec Courtelis

Palm Beach Chairman

Mrs. Mary Sanford

Polo Co-Chairmen

Mrs. Helen Boehm   Mr. William Ylvisaker

Board of Directors

Mr. Arthur B. Krim
Chairman

Mrs. Anna Bing Arnold	Mr. John Kluge
Mr. Alec P. Courtelis	Mrs. Patricia Kluge
Mrs. Louise Courtelis	Mrs. Della Koenig
Mrs. Oscar Getz	Ms. Sherry Lansing
Mrs. Diane Glazer	Dr. Theodore D. Lockwood
Mr. Guilford Glazer	Dr. Martin Meyerson
Mr. Arthur Groman	Mrs. Abigail Phillips
Mrs. Miriam Groman	Mr. Anthony Portago
Dr. Armand Hammer	Mr. B. Francis Saul II
Mrs. Frances Hammer	Miss Rosemary Tomich
Mr. Paul C. Hebner	Mrs. Jane Weintraub
Dr. Ray R. Irani	Mr. Jerry Weintraub
Mrs. Sandra Hoover Jordan	Mr. Kemal Zeinal-Zade

The **second** invitation concerned a gala luncheon and polo match to be held at the Palm Beach Polo and Country Club the same day -- also "in the presence of Their Royal Highnesses."

In the **third** invitation, Dr. and Mrs. Hammer invited us to a black-tie party at the Norton Gallery the preceding evening. It coincided with the grand opening of their magnificent art collection.

The Missing Link

It dawned upon us that one item had <u>not</u> been included in THE envelope: a request for $10,000 (per couple) as patrons of the United World Colleges. Clearly, this was not an oversight, but an expression of gratitude to the gracious and helpful Mayor across the lake.

This scenario triggered an interesting "Eureka experience." It concerned my joking reference over the years about Carol having "a touch of royalty." This perception had now been validated by world-class authorities on the subject.

Section II

EVENTS AT THE NORTON GALLERY OF ART

I have always said that any news reporter who is not fascinated by the rich and famous is not a good news reporter.

Clifton Daniel
(*The Miami Herald*
June 27, 1984, p. B-3)

10

The Norton Gallery Exhibit

A black-tie reception at the Norton Gallery of Art honoring the Armand Hammer Collection, *Five Centuries of Masterpieces*, constituted the first major event in this two-day societal whirlwind. Admission was by special invitation to guests attending The Ball the following evening, and to persons intimately involved with the Gallery. Occidental Petroleum Company representatives made the arrangements for this bonus to benefactors of the United World College of the American West. The list of guests who would view the fabulous collection, however, was kept secret for security reasons.

A humorous episode highlighted the exclusivity of this event. Richard Madigan, Director of the Gallery, initially had not been invited to the dinner! *The Palm Beach Post* (November 9, 1985, p. A-1) noted: "He was only invited after they were embarrassed into it."

En Route

Charlotte Mitchell had been our housekeeper for more than two decades. As she left home that Monday morning, Carol left Charlotte a note: "We'll be dining out today and tomorrow." She was almost tempted to add the tease "...with Royalty."

Driving to the Norton Gallery of Art, I reflected on an extraordinary association. We had attended a wonderful concert by Neil Sedaka and his group at the West Palm Beach Auditorium the previous night. One of his ballads began, "Girl, we reached the top..." This sentiment erupted onto my conscious level as I reflexively turned to gaze at Mayor Carol Roberts.

A doorman took our car. We happened to arrive the same time as Gregory Peck and his wife Veronique. Recognizing the movie star, I introduced him to Mayor Carol Roberts. A woman then rushed up and asked "Greg" if he would introduce us. Before he could do so, Peck was besieged by photographers.

This encounter was resurrected by our dinner companions at The Ball next night while conversing with Carol.

Guest: "What do you think of Joan Collins?" (This British-born actress played a cunning *femme fatale* in the popular TV series *Dynasty*.)
Carol: "I don't watch much television, and therefore wouldn't know what she looks like."
Guest: "Really?"
Carol: "Really!"
Guest: "Well, she's sitting only one-arm length away from your husband... over there."
Carol: "What do you know? That's the same woman who asked Gregory Peck if he would introduce us to her!"

The Hammer Collection

Five Centuries of Masterpieces was an impressive collection of more than 100 masterworks of Western European and American art. The exhibition contained 18 new acquisitions since its prior showing in 1980 -- including paintings by Rembrandt, Titian, Tintoretto, Chardin and Watteau. Indeed, this was reputed to be the most sought-after private art collection in the world.

The Roberts <u>really</u> were interested in viewing the collection. In addition to collecting art, we had visited many of the leading museums in the world.

As an unexpected fringe benefit, we again encountered Gregory Peck in one of the galleries. Carol then discussed several paintings as she and Peck walked around the room... to the delight of several photographers who detected them (see Photo Section).

Having received so much flak from some Palm Beach socialites, Dr. Hammer and his colleagues got in the last word. It was a full-page ad in the November 16, 1985 edition of the *Palm Beach Daily News* ("the Shiny Sheet") announcing: "The Armand Hammer Collection: Five Centuries of Masterpieces: <u>Now On View</u>." The crowds it attracted broke all previous records. There were 1,200 and 1,400 visitors at the Gallery, respectively, the first two days. (Previously, 500 had been considered a giant turnout.)

Subsequent revelations about Hammer's intent in acquiring famous works of art appear in Chapter 24. Stated bluntly, they were to be his "ticket to immortality."

11

The Norton Gallery Reception/Dinner

The Reception

We encountered many notables from the United States and abroad at the Norton Gallery reception. They included our two congressmen and Senator Paula Hawkins. *The Evening Times* characterized the reception as "a curious mixture of high-octane premium laced with a liberal dollop of crude" (November 13, 1985, p. C-1). (Neither the Royal Couple nor Dr. Armand Hammer were in town for this opening.)

Media mogul Ted Turner and his wife Jane (see Photo Section) chatted with us at length. Ted recalled Carol from their battle over his baseball-team franchise a decade earlier. (She had cast the single dissenting vote.) Turner was elated to meet Gregory Peck. He took someone's seat at the actor's table to tell him that he had seen *Duel in the Sun* 30 times!

We didn't recognize most of the guests... but weren't the only ones. Billionaire H. Ross Perot entered the Norton Gallery of Art, looked around, and said to a stranger: "Excuse me, we're from Dallas, and we don't know anybody here" (*The Palm Beach Post* November 12, 1985, p. A-12).

Friends, both old and new, were intrigued by Carol's recent experiences in East Africa, especially Ted Turner. They expressed admiration for this humanitarian venture, particularly on learning that she and a few others had set up a private foundation -- Assisting Communities to Self Help (ACTS) -- for achieving their goals.

Carol also engaged Warren Edward Avis (of rental car fame) in a fascinating discussion that included the psychology of political leadership.

The Dinner

Our table (#6) included guests from Germany, France, Canada and Yugoslavia. We really didn't know who they were until their titles appeared in newspapers the next day. They consisted of Duchess Elaine de Montesquieu, Paul Louis Weiller, Dr. Kurt Schwarzbach (chairman of a major German engineering/construction company), and the Prince of Yugoslavia. The latter introduced himself as merely "a recent Palm Beach resident."

A delicious dinner was served, along with the appropriate wines and champagne. A humorous incident occurred at our table when one of the other guests mistook the expensive wrap of my adjacent dinner companion for a napkin!

The charm of the West Palm Beach Mayor, coupled with more accounts of her recent visit to Africa, captivated our dinner partners. We departed, bidding each other: "Good night. See you tomorrow at The Ball."

This occasion of farewells yielded a delightful bonus for one of our Palm Beach friends. She attended the dinner as an officer of the Norton Museum. When a newly-made acquaintance at her table bid her adieu, he expressed the anticipated pleasure of seeing her at The Ball. She informed him that she wasn't coming because no invitation had been received. The following morning, she and her husband received a hand-delivered invitation.

Section III

ROYAL TRIVIA

There must be more to life than having everything..

Maruice Sondak

12

Royal Confessions of a Political Spouse

Let me be frank: I had paid <u>minimal</u> attention to accounts of Bonny Prince Charles and Princess "Di" prior to Carol's involvement in planning for their visit. The media and politicians, however, repeatedly made negative general comments about royalty. For instance, Senator William Cohen of Maine asserted that the purchase of $640 toilet seats for aircraft by the Pentagon "gives new meaning to the word 'throne'."

My attitude underwent an extraordinary transformation after we received the foregoing invitations requesting the pleasure of our company "in the Presence of Their Royal Highnesses." The intensity of such interest mushroomed once the Royal Couple arrived in Washington for a reception by President and Mrs. Reagan.

- It became nearly impossible to read local newspapers and national periodicals without encountering at least one feature about the Prince and the Princess.
- I had been intrigued by Dr. Armand Hammer for many years. This physician-capitalist-philanthropist was still going strong in his 80s. In addition, I had been the personal physician of his brother (Victor) and his sister-in-law while they resided in Palm Beach.
- I was motivated to brush up on proper etiquette to avoid making an embarrassing boo-boo.

As the date for arrival of the Royal Couple approached, Carol and I suspected that we would be minor pawns in a media-created event. But we reasoned, "Why not enjoy this Royal Vaudeville featuring the globe's most scrutinized couple?" Carol expressed particular interest in the costume changes of these world-class illusionists.

Pre-arrival Experiences and Perspectives

A Change of Plans

The three invitations (Chapter 9) forced me to alter my schedule drastically, especially for the luncheon and polo match. They occurred on a Tuesday... generally a <u>very</u> busy day in my office.

Carol mentioned to several friends the possibility that I might not be going. In short order, <u>five</u> C.E.O.s offered to be her escort -- as well as a dozen professional women wishing to come as her "secretary." Their visions of brushing with royalty were dashed, however, by my rearranged schedule. I jokingly added: "I'm sure that any patient having a semi-emergency wouldn't mind going to Wellington for a royal medical visit."

A Déjà Vu

The return of Prince Charles evoked a personal déjà vu. His first visit during 1980 culminated in a brief hospitalization at the Good Samaritan Hospital after he experienced heat exhaustion during a polo match on April 4. (The heat on the field that day was reported to be so intense that even the horses were given Gatorade.) Charles was put in a room adjacent to one of my patients.

Years later, Terry Rowe, a police officer and the son of a medical colleague, informed me that he had driven the collapsed Prince to the Good Samaritan Hospital.

I never before saw the likes of the fervent pleading and furious bidding among nurses for afternoon and evening duty on that floor... or since. Some were willing to barter entire off-duty weekends for the opportunity to serve just one shift.

The pinnacle of excitement, however, involved <u>my</u> patient. As the Prince prepared to leave, he waved at her. Fortunately, she suffered no relapse of her heart attack from this social shock.

After his recovery from feeling "knackered" (English slang for exhausted), the Prince attended a private party at the Polo Club. He allegedly danced with "lovely ladies well past midnight."

What <u>really</u> impressed the Prince about this unanticipated sojourn? He commented: "Palm Beach -- how could I forget Palm Beach? I passed out and was hospitalized. It's also hard to forget that when I got the bill, I nearly passed out again" (*Palm Beach Daily News* November 6, 1985, p. P-1).

More Professional Encounters

Several extraordinary situations arose that required extreme tact with my Palm Beach patients.

- An 81-year-old socialite listed in *The Blue Book* made me take a virtual oath when she learned I was going to The Ball. She commanded: "You must remember EVERYTHING that happens since you are <u>the only one</u> I know who is actually going to be there!" Considering the many elite social spheres within which she orbited, this plea left me nearly speechless.
- The extreme security precautions at the airport will be described later. They led to an embarrassing encounter at the entry door with one of my Palm Beach patients who didn't have a pass. She accosted me, demanding that I "identify" her so that she could enter. Taken aback, I explained that we had enough of a challenge identifying ourselves.

Springing The Secret

Neither Carol nor I had <u>ever</u> set the merry-go-round of "high society" as personal goals. The recognition of this fact by my Palm Beach patients was conducive to better physician-patient relationships. It also explained my avoiding any mention of THE invitation. Having made a copy for Carol's mother, however, I kept another on my desk... just in case.

One October day proved particularly hectic. I was running an hour behind schedule when an impatient Palm Beacher entered my office. Trying to catch up on dictation about prior patients, I sought some way to humor this socialite. Handing her the invitation, I stated: "You might find this of passing interest." I regret not being able to photograph the expression of disbelief on her face the next five seconds. Her response said it all: "YOU got an invitation?"

As the interview progressed, there was no question about oneupmanship at bridge tables across the lake regarding "<u>my</u> invited doctor."

13

A Crash Course on Royal Manners

Persons knowledgeable about etiquette kept providing the public with advice in the event of a chance encounter with the Royal Couple. Some examples:

- Men should make a slight bow.
- Ladies might perform a slight curtsey... the right foot behind the left foot.
- Avoid "aggressive socializing" and chattering.
- Avoid staring at the couple.
- Positively no cutting-in or dancing with the Princess.
- Positively no autographs.
- Avoid interrupting when Their Royal Highnesses spoke.

The Official Line

Mayor Carol Roberts received these <u>official</u> recommendations from the British Embassy relative to behavior and conversation in greeting the Royal Couple.

- <u>Bowing and Curtseying</u>
  Bowing/curtseying is normal practice for Britons. For Americans it is, of course, entirely optional. The gesture need not be elaborate -- for men a slight inclination of the head, for women a slight bending of the knees.
- <u>Handshaking</u>
  The first move ought to be made by the Prince/Princess of Wales.
- <u>Address</u>
  "Your Royal Highness" is the correct form of initial address; thereafter "Sir" or "Ma'am" (pronounced Mam).
- <u>Conversation</u>
  The Prince and Princess of Wales should initiate a conversation at social events.
- <u>Dress</u>
  Wearing gloves or hats is not mandatory... entirely a matter of personal preference.
- <u>Cameras</u>
  Only official or press photographers are permitted to photograph the Prince and Princess of Wales at close quarters during the visit. No other cameras would be allowed into the immediate vicinity of events attended by Their Royal Highnesses.
- <u>Title</u>
  The correct title of the Princess of Wales is "Her Royal Highness the Princess of Wales". She should NOT be called Princess Diana.

No-nos

These specific no-nos filtered down to us.

- Never refer to these dignitaries as "Chuck" or "Di" in their presence. The Princess felt particularly antagonistic to the latter nickname. (Referring to Queen Elizabeth by her childhood name, Lillibet, would be even more revolting.) The accepted affectionate reference to the Prince by close friends was "Charlie."
- "Strictly personal" questions were forbidden. (To the best of my knowledge, no one embarrassed the Princess by asking her if she was pregnant.)
- Tiaras were not to be worn at The Ball unless the woman had a proper claim to nobility. The *Palm Beach Daily News* summed the matter: "That's royal head-dress, ladies. Save your tiaras for another party" (November 4, 1985, p. 1).

Other Personal Researches and Perspectives

A. Carol had been unexpectedly sensitized to the matter of proper titles, having recently returned from a relief mission to Africa where she was routinely addressed as "Your Worship."

B. As an endocrinologist, I had to think twice on hearing the acronym TRH for "Their Royal Highnesses." In my domain, it usually meant "thyroid releasing hormone."

C. An extraordinary coincidence confronted me on Tuesday, November 5. The *Palm Beach Daily News* carried a feature dealing with the proper way to address the Prince and the Princess. It quoted Mary Jane McCaffrey, a Palm Beach resident, who had co-authored the book, *Protocol: The Complete Handbook of Diplomatic, Official and Social Usage* (published by Devon Publishing Company, Washington, D.C.) She had served as Social Secretary at the White House, and also in the Office of the Chief of Protocol. "The Shiny Sheet" even suggested that guests attending The Ball stow it in the powder room that night.

Several hours later, I saw Mr. Harry Monroe, a longstanding patient. Without knowing that I had been invited to this affair, he handed me a flyer of *Protocol* with the comment: "You might be interested in this, Doctor." It turned out that Mary Jane McCaffrey was his wife!

D. While researching the topics of royalty and manners, I chanced upon a reference by Oliver Goldsmith to "the twelve good rules, the royal game of goose" in *The Deserted Village* (line 232). *Bartlett's Familiar Quotations* ascribed these rules to Charles I. They entailed the following:

- Urge no healths.
- Profane no divine ordinances.
- Touch no state matters.
- Reveal no secrets.
- Pick no quarrels.
- Make no comparisons.
- Maintain no ill opinions.
- Keep no bad company.
- Encourage no vice.
- Make no long meals.
- Repeat no grievances.
- Lay no wagers.

I felt more compassion and respect for Prince Charles if he had assumed the yoke of these ancestral yardsticks.

E. I received an unexpected lesson on "Small Points On Table Etiquette" near Auckland (New Zealand). Paper placetops at the Colliery Room detailed table manners to those seeking "innate refinement." They stressed quiet eating and drinking, the proper and noiseless use of napkins, and the correct use of silverware. The writer also denounced these mannerisms and deficiencies:

- "The affected way" in which some women hold their knife half-way down its length
- The buttering of bread in mid-air, and then held in front of the face to be gouged
- The carrying of food to the mouth on one's knife
- The picking of one's teeth at the table
- The pouring of coffee or tea down one's throat like water being poured out of a pitcher

Input from Palm Beach

The Matter of Titles

The way of addressing European royalty properly generated some humorous input from Palm Beachers. This subject happened to be raised while in the company of a friend who had lived next to members of the last royal family in a central European country. She recalled her own apprehension over being unable to locate the proper designation for the senior member after receiving an invitation to meet him. In desperation, she sought advice from his children's nanny.

Friend:	"What do I call him?"
Nanny:	"He is addressed as 'Your Grace'."
Friend:	"Oh?"
Nanny:	"How long have you known him?"
Friend:	"I met him only once before."
Nanny:	"After you've been with him one day, just call him 'Sonny'."

More on Titles

Some Palm Beachers take all titles seriously. To illustrate the point, a Palm Beach patient had a screaming fit on entering my office as she waved the February 13, 1986 edition of *The Palm Beacher*. Pointing to the cover page, she exclaimed: "You ought to sue for failure to honor your title!" I found a picture of Mayor Carol Roberts and myself in the company of Palm Beach Mayor Deedy Marix and Mr. & Mrs. John Christlieb. It had been taken at the Blue and White Ball benefitting the Graham-Eckes Palm Beach Academy. Why the commotion? I was referred to as "Mr." rather than "Dr."

The "historical paradox" wherein United States citizens buy titles, or obtain them through marriage, was considered in Chapter 2. This activity continues to excite entrepreneurs, as evidenced by the popularity of royal titles auctioned through the Manorial Society of Great Britain, Sotheby's and Strutt & Parkers. The sellers of manor lordships may need money, or seek to avoid high government taxes. Most are not humiliated by parting only with a title -- especially if they have several others.

- Bought titles can be acquired for as little as $7,000 or as much as $700,000 (*The Miami Herald* June 12, 1996, p. D-3).
- Including the word "of" in such titles (e.g., Lord of Wimbledon) is mandatory by British standards. The designation of Lord without it indicates entitlement to a seat in the House of Lords, which goes to a hereditary peer.

Some titled Britishers make personal fund-raising business trips to Palm Beach and elsewhere in search of guests for their upscale ancestral homes. Spencer Compton, the Seventh Marquess of Northampton, illustrates the matter.

> This 49-year-old gentleman came to Palm Beach with Lady Northampton as part of a nationwide tour promoting Castle Ashby, his ancestral home (*Palm Beach Daily News* March 4, 1996, p. 1). It is in the Northampton countryside amid 25 square miles of land, parks, gardens and woods owned by his family for centuries. Indeed, Yardley Chase, a large park on its grounds, was installed in 1087 by Judith, niece of William the Conqueror. Other nearby attractions are Stratford and Princess Diana's ancestral home (Althorp)... only six miles away (Chapter 30).
>
> One can comprehend the fascination of this 100-room castle by well-heeled Palm

Beachers seeking history-themed weekends, and high-level executives desiring a private corporate retreat. Five full-time gardeners and a world-class chef are on the premises. The pursuits of English country life involve archery, skeet shooting, croquet, fishing, carriage driving, horseback riding, and viewing 1,000 head of sheep.

Other in-house attractions include centuries-old books (17,000 from <u>before</u> 1600), Old Master paintings, priceless tapestries and valuable porcelains. Guests can better appreciate these amenities from weekend lectures by experts representing Sotheby's and Christie's.

The Comptons themselves do not reside on the premises. They moved to "an older, smaller house" about 100 miles away, also owned by the family. This 80-room edifice was built 32 years before Columbus discovered the New World!

Et Tu, Rolls Royce?

A heinous deed off Palm Beach on September 27, 1985 vexed both the Royal Couple and Parliament. It was the deliberate dumping of a Rolls Royce, the quintessential symbol of automotive excellence, by a local hairdresser aimed at satisfying the curiosity of divers.

Considering the pampering of some 100,000 Rolls Royce motorcars since 1904, this event became analogous to destroying a sacred icon. Prince Charles and Princess Diana reportedly were furious over such sacrilegious treatment of a major symbol of British honor and prestige.

14

More Royal Trivia

With the imminent arrival of the Royal Couple, the Greater Palm Beach area developed a fascination for Royal Trivia. This necessitated brushing up on Great Britain and English history (see below). King George III, in whose reign the colonists declared their independence, became one focal point.

The Union Flag is commonly known as the Union Jack because it was flown from the jack staff of naval vessels. Its emblems include the crosses of the patron saints of its three countries -- St. George for England; St. Andrew for Scotland; St. Patrick for Ireland.

The thirst for information about Prince Charles, Princess Diana, and the rest of the Royal Family proved insatiable. For example, the press made much of differences in their dance and music preferences; the Prince liked opera, while Diana preferred rock.

The associated sensationalist fodder expanded. Considering that gossip represents a built-in occupational hazard for the Royal Family (Chapters 27 and 28), this was understandable. As a scientist intent upon the facts, I realized that many items generated by local and international rumormongers are best discounted or ignored.

Generalities

This realm of "Trivia Pursuit" clarified some heretofore-vague details. There are five divisions of British nobility: Duke, Marquess, Earl, Viscount and Baron -- with appropriate feminized versions for their wives. Moreover, the children of sovereigns are addressed by the prefix "The."

When the British Royal Family assumed the name of Windsor in 1917, Prince Louis renounced both his prior title and the German name of Battenberg, and adopted the anglicized Mountbatten. He subsequently received the title of Earl Mountbatten of Burma for services rendered during the war and in India.

Historically, the English monarchy is the world's oldest royal institution. It began in the year 829 when King Egbert united the country. Except for an 11-year period in the 1600s, his descendants have remained its kings and queens. The function of contemporary British royalty remains strictly ceremonial, however, even though the Queen is "to be informed, to be consulted, and to be warned."

Princes of Wales had visited the United States for over a century. In 1860, Prince Edward (son of Queen Victoria) became the first royal heir to view the former colonies.

The abdication of Edward The Eighth, subsequently the Duke of Windsor (Chapter 2), has been attributed primarily to concern by the Establishment -- especially the Conservative majority in the House of Commons -- over the prospect of an American-born and twice-divorced Queen. Other issues at the time proved equally relevant. One was the King's known concern ("something must be done") for jobless Welsh miners.

In point of fact, there was no law or constitutional provision against his marrying a commoner or anyone else approved by Parliament. But Edward had to contend with the Statute of Westminster (passed by Parliament in 1931) and the intangible "nonconformist conscience"... the barometer of public behavior as viewed by respectable chapel-going members of the middle and workings classes. The document contained a clause fatal for the King: "Any alteration in the law touching the succession of the Throne or the Royal Style and Titles shall hereafter require the assent of the Parliament of the United Kingdom as well as the Parliaments of all the Dominions."

Mayor Carol Roberts was hardly impressed with these and other details of my newly-acquired knowledge. She expressed little interest about the living arrangements of the Royal Couple at Kensington Palace (also referred to as K.P.) She did take note, however, that King George I really meant "kitchen patrol" when he added cooking rooms in the Palace.

The Prince

Prince Charles stayed at the Nixon White House during his first visit to the United States in 1970.

Few would question that Palm Beach is a symbol of American corporate wealth, being inhabited by some of the country's most successful capitalists. In the light of his own background and rearing, many suspected that Prince Charles was uniquely fascinated by this area.

First, his association with the actual handling of money or the payment of bills was minimal.

Second, he had only minor involvement in capitalistic ventures that entailed his personal wealth. The Prince's involvement subsequently expanded into an international conglomerate to assist charities. He announced a new herbal soft-drink business with the Coca-Cola Company and Schweppes Beverages Ltd. concerning the production and distribution of fruits raised on royal estates. (They were called Duchy No. 1 and Duchy No. 3.)

Third, the Royal Family allegedly held a schizoid attitude concerning whether certain bills would be paid by the government -- most notably those involved with living at Buckingham Palace and Windsor Castle -- or out of private income.

- Queen Elizabeth, his mother, had an ingrained sense of thrift, such as minimizing the waste of electricity in her homes at Balmoral and Sandrangham. When the temperature dropped in these private residences, she purportedly commanded: "If you're cold, put on a pullover" (*The Palm Beach Post* November 6, 1985, p. C-1).
- It was rumored that the Prince used toothpaste sparingly.
- Prince Charles purportedly had a chauffeur deliver his own wine from Buckingham Palace to a restaurant the day before taking his staff out for Christmas lunch.
- The Prince nearly considered giving up polo when someone failed to remove the bill for hay (at 40 pounds a ton) from his mail.

Idiosyncrasies

Prince Charles' alleged idiosyncrasies encompassed vegetarianism, communing with dead relatives (particularly his late uncle, Lord Mountbatten) on a ouija board, and dabbling in folk or alternative medicine. The latter is now not considered so farfetched by many.

The Matter of Height

Prince Charles was one-half inch shorter than the Princess. *Life* Magazine reported that Diana was pleased to dance with a taller partner (Clint Eastwood). The Prince countered with an astute observation: "Marriage is not an up-or-down issue. It's a side-by-side one."

On Clothes

Diana purportedly had much input in sprucing the Prince's image. It became clear that "the Prince proposes, but Diana disposes." Her "gentle persuasion" focused on wearing brighter ties and less somber suits. The prominence of his ear lobes also had to be considered by the royal barber.

Even so, Prince Charles ran a distant last in terms of sartorial style... at least in the eyes of some professing expertise within this realm. Jane Woldridge of *The Miami Herald* found his "downright stodgy" suits quite extraordinary -- especially in light of being only a stone's throw from some of the world's finest tailors on Saville Row. She offered the Prince and his tailor these suggestions (November 6, 1985, p. D-1):

- Go with the sleeker, more European cut suits -- emphasis shoulder pads -- in order to impart a less austere look.

- Replace the "perfectly dull" fabrics (especially striped suits) with subtle, but colorful, plaids and tweeds.
- Try shirts of a color other than white... and hopefully colorful ties.
- Avoid oversized bow ties that tend to make the "generous ears seem larger."
- Loosen up with "a natty blazer, sweater vest or cardigan for plane trips and visits to the coal mines."

Woldridge concluded: "But 36 years is long enough for a single style; it is time, dear fellow, for a change. Tally ho!"

On "The Common Language"

Prince Charles' views about "the common language" riled some persons in the United States. He insisted that "English English" is the only proper way to preserve the language because of the "very corrupting" American version (*The Miami Herald* March 24, 1995, p. A-1).

I found affirmation of this attitude in a surprising place: an address to the Chicago Medical College by Dr. Edmund Andrews published 100 years ago in the *Journal of the American Medical Association* (Volume 25, pages 733-734, 1895). It was titled, "Do Not Let Your Latin Spoil Your English." Andrews stated:

> The master of good style, James Russell Lowell, laments our inferiority to English writers in the respect. He says; "It has long seemed to me that the great vice of American writing and speaking is a studied want of simplicity. Very few American writers wield their native language with the directness, force and precision that are common as the day in the mother country..."
>
> "Short Anglo Saxon words of common use are the best, wherever they will express the meaning! It is this choice of short words, resulting in a condensed style of singular force, which gives the writings of Shakespeare and the English translation of the Bible much of their tremendous power."[1]

Princess Diana

The public seemed far more interested in Princess Diana, now the equivalent of the "Queen of Hearts," than any other member of the royal family. There were numerous innuendos, such as her alleged boredom... an issue that would rear itself in years to come (Chapters 28 and 30).

Family History

Many boned up on the Spencers, Diana's family. They traced their lineage back to 1603 in Saxon England, and were descendants of Oliver Cromwell. As such, they are related to John Churchill, the first Duke of Marlborough, hero of the Battle of Blenheim.

- Five of Diana's ancestors apparently were mistresses of English kings.
- Her grandmother died in New York during 1947.
- Dame Barbara Cartland, her step-grandmother, had been a prolific writer of romantic fiction.
- Princess Diana was supposedly a distant relative of nine presidents of the United States -- from George Washington (Chapter 30) to Ronald Reagan.
- Similarly, distant cousins were galore. They included The Marquis de Sade, Humphrey Bogart, Ben Bradley (Executive Editor of *The Washington Post*), Senator Alan Cranston, the wife of Supreme Court Justice Byron White, and even Herman Goering.

References to British History

Many heads nodded in agreement about a particular joke: Princess Diana representing a "payback" for English women since Anne Boleyn (Chapter 30). This second wife of King Henry VIII was committed by him to the Tower of London -- and subsequently beheaded -- on the charge of adultery with various men, including her brother.

But Diana had one undisputed claim to fame: the first English woman in 300 years to marry an heir to the British throne. The initial royal heirloom she received was a tiara commissioned by Queen Mary (wife of King George V). It contained 19 large pearls suspended below lover's knots of diamonds.

Likes and Dislikes

The press kept the world posted with a barrage of commentaries about Diana's alleged likes, dislikes and behavior. Here are a few samplings:

- The Princess reportedly disliked the three "musts" for Britain's rich -- hunting, shooting and fishing. Her husband made some appropriate accommodations.
- Some of Charles' preferences rubbed off on Diana... at least in the matter of eating less meat. In a television interview, she indicated: "Anyway, fish is cheaper."
- Perhaps the Prince's preference for slim blondes explained his wife's fervor about exercising, dieting and suspected bulimia (forced vomiting) (Chapters 30 and 31).

Another endearing aspect of Princess Diana's visits was the noninflammatory nature of her presence. She seemed to heed the list of suggested topics "for small talk for any occasion" in *Letitia Baldridge's Complete Guide to Executive Manners*.

The Fashion Princess

The Princess Diana's model figure and fantastic gowns overwhelmed many American women... and more than a few men. The Princess was five feet, ten inches... without heels. With heels, which she enjoyed wearing, she towered over her husband. Diana's gracious stance developed in part from her love for ballet dancing. (She had won an award during a 1976 competition.)

Reporters suggested that the cost-conscious Prince fumed over the fortune allegedly spent on Diana's wardrobe. On the other hand, she received many clothes free or at a marked discount. These gestures reflected gratitude for having been the superstar model who singlehandedly revived Britain's dormant fashion industry. The wardrobe of the Princess and its impact on fashion are discussed in Chapters 19 and 29.

There seemed to be no happy medium for Diana concerning clothes. One variable observed by the "Royal Rat Pack" of tabloid reporters was an apparent correlation between the length of her dresses and her mood. Although criticized over their alleged high costs, the same scandal sheets subsequently accused her of recycling outfits... even when wearing such "rags" many months apart and considerable distances away.

> An admirer noticed that Princess Diana was wearing an outfit previously worn to Birmingham, England. She replied: "Well, I'm on an economy drive right now" (*Newsweek* December 20, 1993, p. 94).

But the curious still wondered about the destination of Diana's costly haute couture clothes, which she rarely wore a third time. She explained: "I give them to my sisters and my girlfriends" (*Parade* Magazine April 16, 1989, p. 21).

Many defended the Princess' position and even her shopping habits. Eva Gabor joked: "If I had her money, I would shop for much more than she does" (*The Palm Beach Post* November 12, 1985, p. A-12).

Letters by a Previous Royal Couple

I paid closer attention to historical letters involving Britain's royal family. The repeated exposure of our community to the Duke and Duchess of Windsor after the former abdicated as King Edward VIII (Chapter 2) heightened such interest.

The letters exchanged by this couple were published following the Duchess' death. These communications reflect profound bitterness against a system that would not let a monarch pursue his private life. There was frequent use of "WE" -- symbolizing their joint first names. They also revealed the emotional frustration inflicted by nobility (*The Palm Beach Post* May 9, 1986, p. A-11).

- A letter by the Duke, dated March 22, 1937, asserted: "God, how I hate and despise the lot... I hope one day to, and I mean to, get back at those swine and at least make them realize how disgustingly and unsportingly they have behaved."
- In a March 6, 1937 letter, the Duchess commented that the British "are a nation of cads where women are concerned."

[1]1995 American Medical Association. Reproduced with permission.

Section IV

THE ARRIVAL

The rich are different from us.

F. Scott Fitzgerald

15

Receiving The Royal Couple

Mayor Carol Roberts informed other members of the West Palm Beach Commission that they would have to conduct the weekly meeting on Tuesday (the previous Monday being Veterans Day) owing to her absence because of "a prior commitment." When told the details, all hands obligingly agreed to delay the meeting until Wednesday.

"The Chauffeur of The Limousine"

Mayor Roberts remained in continual communication with Michael Hewitt, the deputy British Consul-General out of Atlanta, concerning arrangements. He told Carol to have her "chauffeur" drive "the limousine" to a special VIP parking area at the north terminal where Charles and Diana would be arriving. She had to restrain her laughter on reflecting that I was the chauffeur, and her limousine my car. But I had no objection with such guaranteed entrance to this "holy of society holies," however brief.

Preliminaries

Security at the airport was extraordinary. Only persons with specific credentials and passes could pass through the doors. By the time the Roberts reached the Butler Aviation Terminal at the Palm Beach International Airport, an eager mob had congregated outside.

Carol and I were ushered to a private area. We met several friends -- including Governor and Mrs. Bob Graham, Mayor "Deedy" Marix of Palm Beach, Ken Adams (Chairman, Palm Beach County Commissioners), and County Administrator John Sansbury. Carol then introduced me to Consul-General Hewitt. Representatives of Occidental Petroleum and the United World Colleges also greeted us.

The private plane of Dr. Armand Hammer arrived shortly thereafter. Carol welcomed him in another room. Hammer asked to meet me when informed that I had doctored his brother and sister-in-law.

Carol and I next received instructions from Miss Sarah Gillett, Third Secretary at the British Embassy in Washington. She described this precise order in the receiving line to greet the Royal Couple.

Robert Graham, Governor of Florida
Mrs. Robert Graham
Mr. Barry Holmes, British Consul-General (Atlanta)
Mrs. Holmes
Mr. Kenneth Adams, Chairman of the Palm Beach County Commission
Mrs. Adams
Mrs. Carol Roberts, Mayor of West Palm Beach
Dr. H.J. Roberts
Mrs. Yvelene Marix, Mayor of Palm Beach
Mr. Nigel Marix
Dr. Armand Hammer
Mrs. Hammer
Mr. John Sansbury, County Administrator
Mrs. Sansbury
Mr. Arthur Hailand, CEO of Butler Aviation
Mrs. Hailand

Fringe Benefits from Her Honor

Others appreciated Mayor Carol Roberts even more for opening the paths of access to view the Royal Couple. She had been able to get 15 such invitations... an extraordinary feat in itself. Each had a special number. Most were given to friends and members of the City Hall staff.

The Mayor also had been asked to invite guests belonging to certain clubs and organizations that fostered links with Britain. She told the press: "I'm calling everyone from the Navy Mothers and the Palm Beach Pipe and Drum Corps to the Scottish American Association" (*News/Sun-Sentinel* October 20, 1985, p. A-17).

The Arrival

As the plane carrying the Royal Couple approached the airport, Miss Gillett marched us to the runway in proper order. The Prince and Princess alighted only ten minutes late... a rather remarkable feat considering their delay at the Washington airport.

Two large platforms had been set up for photographers and cameramen hailing from around the world. (Security cleared about 500 members of the media documenting the event.) They remained glued to their positions for nearly three hours, having received this command concerning their positions: "Once you select your spot, you may not move!"

Standing in the receiving line, I recalled a remark that seemed appropriate in anticipation of meeting Princess Diana. It was President John F. Kennedy's one-liner: "I'm the man who accompanied Jacqueline Kennedy to Paris."

Considering the stiff breeze, we were grateful that the Prince and Princess didn't dilly-dally at the plane's open door. The pair's brisk walk down the steps reminded one reporter of commuters on the New York shuttle. Carol tried to secure her hat with a pin, but found the effort hopeless. (Princess Diana encountered the same difficulty.)

As the Royal Couple approached, I kept reminding myself about their proper titles, and the "must not touch" admonition. The latter proved no problem. The Prince held out his hand to Carol, who shook it... and repeated the same gesture with me (see Photo Section). The Princess did likewise.

A goof by President Reagan several days previously kept all hands alert. He forgot to include Diana's official title. Reagan then really put his foot in his mouth by referring to her as "Princess David" and "Princess Dianne." The director of *Burke's Peerage*, a bible of British Bluebloods, likened this fumble by "the Gipper" to Queen Elizabeth II being called "Libby" (*The Miami Herald* November 11, 1985, p. A-1).

After extending greetings from the City of West Palm Beach, Mayor Roberts engaged the Prince in a prolonged conversation. Nearly everyone viewing this encounter, both there and on television, expressed surprise at the dialogue's duration. Carol was besieged by reporters -- and later by her mother -- concerning the word-for-word details of this conversation. Here it is:

Prince: "Are you going to attend the ball?"
Carol: "I sure am! I wouldn't miss it for the world!"
Prince: "My, you're a brave one!"
Carol: "That's all right with me."

This exchange provided clear evidence of the Prince's awareness that the visit had ruffled more than a few Palm Beacher feathers.

The highlight for me, of course, was Carol meeting the Princess. Several photographers captured this long-to-be-remembered moment (see Photo Section).

The warmth and cordiality of the Prince and the Princess proved disarming. I conjectured to the British Deputy Consul-General that this climax of their trip probably came as fun after the three-day ordeal with Washington formality. He agreed.

The Princess received numerous flowers. Tara, daughter of County Administrator John Sansbury, could hardly restrain herself when presenting Diana with a bouquet of flowers (see Photo Section). The Princess' winning way with children became apparent.

Anglophiles on both sides of the fence strained to catch glimpses of the Royal Couple. Many in the crowd waved American flags and Union Jacks. School children had been told they might be seeing the future King of England.

Another remarkable sight caught my attention: unloading 7,000 pounds of royal luggage. Moreover, the Prince was accompanied by his valet, butler, baggage master, gentleman-in-waiting, private detectives, personal secretary (with whom we were to have lunch at Wellington), and press secretary.

The Billiard Connection

Milton Klein, Carol's father, had to be hospitalized two days before the Royal Couple arrived. As I left his room before heading to the airport, Milton offered this surprising revelation: "Tell the Prince that I used to play billiards with his Uncle, Prince Albert, when he visited Miami." At the time, Milton was considered one of the top amateur billiard players in the country.

Another Long Conversation

The lengthy conversation between the Prince and Nigel Marix, husband of Palm Beach Mayor "Deedy" Marix, impressed many persons. Intrigued by the nature of this animated discussion, they sought details.

Nigel's tie proved to be the focus of mutual interest. Charles promptly recognized the Royal Air Force colors. Nigel indicated that he had served as a pilot in the R.A.F. during and after World War II. Furthermore, his father was Air Vice Marshall R.L.G. Marix, who distinguished himself during both world wars.

"Reggie" appears to have been the first pilot in history to have effectively bombed a target in enemy territory. On last-minute orders from Winston Churchill, he destroyed a brand new zeppelin in Dusseldorf. This daring feat occurred as the Germans entered Antwerp. The details can be found in *Reggie: The Life of Air Vice Marshall RLG Marix CB DSO* by John Lea (The Pentland Press Limited).

16

Polo Anyone?

The public had been repeatedly warned against coming to the airport to view the Royal Couple because of anticipated congestion and the need for considerable security. But this effort was for naught. A mob intercepted us on returning to our car.

We finally were able to depart for the Palm Beach Polo and Country Club, and took a route other than the one the caravan of limousines probably would be taking. Even so, many persons waited along the way, cameras in hand, to catch a glimpse of Prince Charles and Princess Diana. They obviously concurred with the remark by The Reverend John Mangrum of Wellington's St. David's in the Pines Episcopal Church: "The Royal Couple should take the damned celebration over here where it belongs (*News/Sun Sentinel* October 20, 1985, p. A-1).

Wellington

Many readers outside our area understandably assumed that the "Palm Beach Polo and Country Club" was in Palm Beach. Several features in the national press and on television contributed to such misunderstanding. Palm Beachers also got in their licks.

- The President of the Palm Beach Chamber of Commerce felt that the word "County" should have been used to designate an establishment 15 miles away.
- Some referred to this insect-infested unincorporated suburb as "Fly Land."

The aura of Palm Beach nevertheless persisted... and does so even now. *The Wall Street Journal* carried this ad, centering about polo, for the Palm Beach Polo and Country Club: "It's not whether you win or lose, but where you play the game" (January 20, 1995, p. B-7).

Suggestions About Clothes

Palm Beach Polo provided some "bare facts" about what one wears to polo for "the spectator sport where everyone can play" (*The Palm Beach Post* December 8, 1985, p. E-8). Women generally opt for slacks or shorts and casual tops, or even sundresses and straw hats. Men wear casual dress pants or shorts, along with a comfortable knit shirt or oxford cloth. Socks are optional... but not for horses on the field.

Here are **some no-nos**:

- Suits, including bathing suits, are out. (So are suits of armor.)
- Neckties are definitely out. ("You're not coming to work; you're coming to play.")
- Fancy jewelry is frowned upon in this setting. ("The only rocks you'll see here are in the drinks at our Polo Cafe.")
- Designer clothes are discouraged. ("You're likely to see more original designers in the crowd than designer originals.")

Historical Perspectives About Polo in the U.S.

Lest the reader believe that polo was imported recently, some apple-pie-loving Americans enjoyed it early this century. Will Rogers had a passion for polo according to Samuel Marx in his book *Broadway Portraits* (Donald Flamm, Inc., New York, 1929, p. 35). Rogers not only owned two polo fields, but also another one for practising.

More On Wellington

The Royal Couple had received a Wellington condominium as a wedding present. The Princess designed it herself.

Diana's sensitivity became evident when she found herself without tip money for the bellman who brought her luggage. She thereupon offered him a six-pack of beer from the well-stocked refrigerator.

Preparations for the Royal Visit were in progress at Wellington over five months. Unfortunately, this famous polo match impacted minimally on local businesses, with several notable exceptions.

> The editor of *The Town-Crier* wondered "where the $5-per-car parking fee went?" Bink Glisson was upset over this charge for parking his car in a nearby lot. He recalled purchasing the land for $10 an acre when putting this 18,000-acre parcel together for the Wellington family (*Palm Beach Daily News* November 13, 1985, p. 1).

A Very Private Luncheon

Security at Wellington was even tighter for the "Gala Luncheon" than at the airport. We were ushered into the clubhouse overlooking the playing fields. Three tables, set for about two dozen persons, of a Brunschwig and Fils fabric printed with birds and flowers. The settings consisted of white china bordered in green.

In addition to the Prince and Princess, there were Dr. Hammer, Governor and Mrs. Bob Graham, the British Ambassador, the Prince's private secretary Sir John Riddell, William Ylvisaker (Chairman of the Polo and Country Club, and a member of "The Palm Beach Team") and his daughter, Jerry Grinberg (President of North American Watch), John O. Grettenberger (Vice President of General Motors, and General Manager of the Cadillac Division), and several young persons with their wives. They introduced themselves as members of the polo team.

Carol was charmed by Memo Gracida, a 10-goaler considered to be one of the world's best polo players. He reminisced about his father playing polo with Prince Charles' father.

All the while, I kept asking Carol: "Where are the others?" We then headed for a special section in the stands where "invited guests" would view the polo match. En route, we passed the other invitees lunching in an enormous tent.

> This "patron tent" seated about 300 persons. It had a fabric ceiling of royal blue chiffon. Table overlays of royal blue and green alternated throughout the tent. The planners had arranged ten benefactors' tables surrounded by white trellises and live greenery. A lavish $27,000 portable toilet accommodated the guests.

The Polo Match

The weather seemed made to order for polo. The stands were mobbed. Another obvious appeal of this event was the opportunity to observe society's "heroes." Several of the celebrities whom we had met the previous evening at the Norton Gallery of Art followed us. They included Merv Griffin, Ted Turner, Eva Gabor, and H. Ross Perot.

When Ken Adams, Chairman of the Palm Beach County Commission, sat next to Carol, it became apparent that polo-tics also would be played.

We enjoyed the match. Persons viewing polo for the first time likened it to watching "horseback hockey."

Only Prince Charles wore a face mask. (One columnist equated it to dressing the quarterback for the Miami Dolphins in a suit of armor.) As important, the Prince had received lots of advice about drinking enough fluid.

Several airborne distractions occurred.

- Local columnist Ron Wiggins of *The Palm Beach Post* had no intention of being upstaged. A plane flew overhead with the message from this tennis buff: "TENNIS TOMORROW, DIANA 471-4361 RON WIGGINS."
- Another plane towed a banner that read: "CHARLES AND DIANA. PLEASE HELP TO FREE IRELAND.

I.A.U.C." The initials stood for the Irish-American Unity Conference, a Texas- based organization promoting the reunification of Ireland. (It had paid $650 for this flight from Davie.) I remarked to several guests from Houston sitting alongside us that this seemed an unfair insult. They agreed. The message apparently did have some impact because this San Antonio group received a number of phone calls from reporters.

The "odd-ball investment" of Ylvisaker clearly had paid off in many ways. This corporate mogul not only turned a profit from the sale of land in Wellington, but had revived the dying sport of polo in the United States. As a fringe benefit, the 61-year-old chap could play polo with the Prince of Wales.

His "Palm Beach Team," which included the Prince, edged "The All Stars" by a score of 11 to 10. But the event proved a win-win on several accounts. At the very least, the Prince's interest in polo, coupled with a beautiful facility, removed this sport from the undeserved receiving end of American jokesters.

17

The Economic Boost

As some Palm Beach socialites yawned over the forthcoming visit of the Royal Couple, merchants on both sides of Lake Worth burned the midnight oil to take advantage of it.

- Persons with diplomatic careers who had retired in the Palm Beaches emphasized "The British Look."
- The Royal Couple would be sleeping on sheets provided by Pioneer Linens in downtown West Palm Beach.
- Palm Beach's Epicurean Restaurant imported strawberries from New Zealand and clotted cream from England for a formal afternoon tea honoring Diana's designer to be held two days after The Ball.
- A host of support personnel flocked to the area. Robin Weier, Nancy Reagan's hairdresser, flew in to work on Joan Collins, Eva Gabor, and other fashionable women.
- Saks Fifth Avenue on Worth Avenue commemorated the visit by displaying white and yellow roses -- the official flowers of Her Royal Highness -- in one of its windows.

The Tiara Thing

The fact that only Princess Diana had the prerogative of wearing a tiara to The Ball (Chapter 13) did not deter the House of Kahn. It threw a cocktail party for about 180 tiara enthusiasts at its Peruvian Avenue establishment. A collection of 12 tiaras was on display.

Although no one purchased a tiara, the owner said: "We did this as a fun thing, as a remembrance of a bygone era" (*Palm Beach Daily News* November 10, 1985, p. A-4).

An irony emerged: Diana was not particularly fond of wearing tiaras.

The Shiny Sheet later offered a full-page feature on "The Top Ten Tiaras" in Palm Beach (October 21, 1996, p. 6)... past and present. It noted that this "crowning glory" refers to "the gem-encrusted little crowns that rest atop those perfect coifs." In addition to Princess Diana, the list included Marjorie Merriweather Post, Ann Light, Eunice Gardiner, Noreen Drexel, Jane Dudley, Yvonne Mills, Marylou Whitney, Barton Gubelmann and Pat Schmidlapp.

My researches on the subject revealed that Eleanor Roosevelt had been the recipient of a 6-inch-high gold tiara... encrusted with colored stones and featuring two birds. Sidi Mohammed, the Sultan of Morocco, presented it to her in 1943. The tiara ultimately ended up in the National Archives... but with no indication if the First Lady had ever worn it to any function.

An Editorial Admonition

Concerned individuals expressed dismay over the community's failure to appreciate this economic windfall.

Philip Lukin editorialized on its unmistakable economic benefits in the November 11 issue of *The Palm Beach Social Pictorial* (p. 4). He pointed out the overflow business for florists, beauty parlors, high-fashion shops, limousine services, and other businesses.

Photographic Opportunities

The cadre of photographers who cover Palm Beach society began salivating. They envisioned high prices for pictures of anyone caught in the company of the Royal Couple or the renowned invitees... especially at The Ball.

Guests began practising their seemingly natural come-hither expressions and "royal bearing" in front of mirrors. This art of the I-have-arrived pose has attained new heights among certain Palm Beach socialites. Some do it instinctively when they even sense the presence of photographers for *The Shiny Sheet* and other "society publications."

The Palm Beach Post (December 13, 1996, F-1) listed the following components of "the pose" for women:

- Smile just enough to turn up the corners of the mouth. Don't grin.
- Keep the head erect with the chin up to enhance an aristocratic air... and smooth wrinkles.
- Angle the shoulders sideways to add definition to the waist.
- Curve the elbow gently unless holding a glass.
- Relax the hands... but not flat against the thigh to avoid appearing nervous.
- Slightly bend and extend one leg, with the heel nestled near the arch of the back foot (comparable to the third position in ballet).
- Point the toes of the extended foot downward, the heel being raised a bit.
- Hold a glass of liquor behind one's back or that of an adjacent person being photographed to avoid later embarrassment. (Use care, however, if the other individual does the same thing.)
- Fluff the dress to make the drapes unencumbered.
- Tilt the purse to prevent this "tummy disguise" from lying flat against the body.

Photographers covering these events have revealed their favorite stories. Mort Kaye recalls bowing to the Prince and Princess after taking a photo of them with Dr. and Mrs. Hammer. Charles responded, "Why did you do that? You're not Japanese" (*The Palm Beach Post* December 13, 1996, p. F-6).

Section V

THE BALL

Wealth and content are not always bedfellows.

Benjamin Franklin
(Poor Richard 1732)

18

Preparations

All hands concerned -- invited guests, The Breakers Hotel, and the Royal Couple -- went into high gear as The Ball approached. Needless to say, many well-known socialites and personalities had every intention of attending this societal bombshell... with or without the presence of hostile Palm Beachers. Several notable coincidences recently occurred at The Breakers and elsewhere in Palm Beach.

- The leaders of Florida's business community had gathered several days previously for the "Council of 100" meeting. Senator Lawton Chiles, invited to discuss the infrastructure of Florida taxes, stated that he had no intention of delaying the visit just to meet royalty. He told the *Palm Beach Daily News* (November 9, 1985, p. 1): "But there's no way I'll be here. I'll be in session at the time, working."
- Former President Richard Nixon walked the corridors of The Breakers only several weeks before... virtually unnoticed. Carl Ronaszeki, the head chef, poignantly commented: "There are rising stars, and there are falling stars" (*The Miami Herald* November 18, 1985, p. C-1).
- Palm Beach has been the site of memorable balls of nearly every description, some quite bizarre. For example, the Young Friends of the Red Cross Ball were nearing completion of plans for its naughtiest charity ball of the year to be held at the Henry Flagler Museum a month after The Ball. (Someone pointed out that persons qualifying for Social Security could still be members of the "junior" committee.) Its previous productions included live elephants, headless Greek statues with television sets perched on their necks, and fake human sacrifices. A "fractured fairy tale theme" was to be enacted by 30 actors dressed as story-book characters. Even this benefit was influenced by the visit of the Royal Couple, as indicated in its invitations issued by "H.R.H. Prince Charming."

Making a Getaway from City Hall

The gala black-tie reception at The Breakers was to begin at 7:30 PM. Mayor Carol Roberts conducted a scheduled planning and zoning hearing late that afternoon. She had always attempted to give discussers enough time to present their views. But this became the one occasion when she refused to tolerate long-winded lawyers. Carol described one such encounter.

Carol: "Put it in writing. That way we'll understand your suggestion better."
Lawyer: "What's the big rush?"
Carol: "A social commitment."
Lawyer: "Like what?"
Carol: "Like meeting the Prince and Princess of Wales at The Ball tonight, which you seem to want
       me to miss!"
Lawyer: "Oh!"

The New Tuxedo

I was confronted with a dilemma on the day of The Ball: the sudden need for a contingency formal outfit. A small tear developed in the left back sleeve of my jacket during the black-tie affair at the Norton Gallery the previous evening.

I brought the jacket to my tailor early that morning. He indicated that it <u>must</u> be picked up by 2 PM because he had a doctor's appointment. Uncertain about being able to do so in time in view of the trip to Wellington, I decided to take no chances and buy another outfit. This proved a memorable excursion (Chapter 21).

Later that evening, I discovered that other invited guests had to make a similar last-minute arrangements for their formal attire. Two executives of Occidental Petroleum -- one from California, and the other from Connecticut -- gave comparable accounts. They received four hours notice about attending The Ball in Palm Beach... along with the command: "Go and buy a formal suit, <u>now</u>!" Each then called his wife with a concurrent command: "Go and buy a new dress, <u>now</u>!"

The Breakers Hotel

The Breakers went to extraordinary lengths in providing glamorous "fall surroundings" for the Royal Couple. Florists and decorators had planned the effects since summer.

- The ballroom was decorated in autumnal colors. Fresh red daisies hung from the vaulted ceiling of the ballroom.
- The centerpieces decorating the tables included lilies, Gerber daisies, and mums in yellow and orange tones.
- Wispy gold-lace cloths covered the tables.
- The china was white and gold.
- The waiters wore white gloves.
- Because only Bollinger Champagne had been served at the wedding of the Prince and Princess, this firm arranged to have the hotel serve it.
- The Breakers purchased a new "Regal Red" carpet to pad the entry of royal footsteps.
- There were highly polished brass stanchions and cords, waxed floors, and polished chandeliers.
- The captains at the hotel received new tuxedos.
- Two hotel valets were dressed as Beefeaters. (Unfortunately, they didn't pass the Prince's inspection. He noted that the arms of the coats "don't quite fit.")
- Helen Boehm, owner of the Boehm Polo Team, planned to give porcelain roses to ladies attending The Ball. She referred to them as "Frances Hammer Roses" in honor of Hammer's wife.
- The Breakers took down its Flagler System flag on the south tower, and replaced it with the Union Jack. (The flag of Florida remained on the north tower.)

Security

Extraordinary security measures were in place. The U.S. Secret Service took charge, notwithstanding the hotel's own security force. The windows facing the ocean were boarded on the night of The Ball. In addition, the British Secret Service, the Palm Beach Police Department, and Occidental Petroleum's private security forces surveyed all entrances, windows and other vulnerable areas.

En Route

I found myself enthralled by some strange déjà vu while dressing, but couldn't fathom it at first. A similar tension had haunted me intermittently over previous weeks, especially on reading accounts of the fabulous costumes that some of the female guests planned to wear.

The answer suddenly hit me at 7 PM, the magic hour on "D-Day": Cinderella's step-sisters preparing for the Prince's ball. Opening the door of our home before departing, I joked to Carol about not finding a magic coach and horsemen waiting for her.

Security on ALL Palm Beach roads was <u>really</u> tight. Some "royal gawkers" had driven hundreds of miles to get a first-hand look at the Royal Couple. We noted police cars stationed every one or two blocks north of the Southern Boulevard bridge. We were allowed to proceed to the entrance at The Breakers only after showing a document with the notation: "Admission by This Card Only."

The international excitement became increasingly evident. Three rows of photographers were positioned to the left of the entrance. Most of the 500 conventioneers attending the Associated General Contractors of North and South Carolina mobbed the lobby.

We FINALLY gained admittance to the reception -- but only after presenting our special card another <u>four</u> times. Several Palm Beach friends, as well as acquaintances met the previous evening at the Norton Gallery of Art, greeted us.

Carol unexpectedly excused herself and hurried to meet a couple... Bob and Dolores Hope. After introducing herself, she said to Bob: "My father told me to remind you that you played billiards together in Cleveland when both of you were about 20. He <u>insisted</u> that I extend his regards." Hope thanked her.

19

An Ultimate in High Fashion

S ome fashion-minded readers might not forgive me if I fail to mention the gowns and embellishments worn by women attending The Ball, especially Princess Diana. Subsequent events related to "the Princess of high fashion" appear in Chapter 29.

The Princess of High Fashion

The Princess of Wales clearly was THE main center of attraction... with particular focus on her wardrobe. As noted earlier, Diana had become fashion's most charismatic personality since Jacqueline Kennedy.

Having observed the Princess in both formal and informal attire, Carol and I were in agreement with designer Geoffrey Beane: "It doesn't matter what she wears. I don't think the clothes are that good, some of the design is not on target to me as a professional, but who cares? Her presence overcomes any banalities of dress" (*The Palm Beach Post* November 22, 1985, p. C-1). The essence boiled down to a lovely person with a model's figure displaying fine taste.

Princess Diana -- five feet ten and a half inches, and a perfect size 8 -- was the dream of photographers and designers. As Britain's national treasure of fashion, "Shy Di" had become transformed into the glamorous *femme fatale* of "Dynasty Di." (Her popularity also was explainable as a post-feminist young lady who had rejuvenated British royalty.) Indeed, Dover Publications published a paperdoll book in which the Princess could be dressed in 23 different ensembles.

Even I was impressed by the extraordinary dimensions of Di-mentia. Some estimated the worth of "Britain's foremost walking mannequin" -- in terms of publicity and actual sales -- as high as $650,000,000 (*People* Magazine November 11, 1985, p. 138). The scheduling of her visit to a J.C. Penney store in suburban Washington D.C. hadn't been a coincidence. This company recently purchased $60 million of British-made sweaters, skirts, dresses, coats, shoes and scarves for its nationwide "Best of Britain" merchandising campaign. The enormous upsurge in hat sales provided another example. (Diana had worn 27 hats between February 1 and August 1, 1985.)

The frequency with which the Princess changed outfits proved mind-boggling. During this same six-month period, she donned at least 74 different costumes while attending 109 events. It was in keeping with an apparent rule: Diana should not wear any garment in public more than six times.

This extraordinary effort entailed the designing of clothes, fittings, a lady-in-waiting, and the assembly of clothes for trips abroad. It required large blocks of time, considerable money, and lots of planning. As a case in point, the wardrobe of the Prince and Princess during an Italian visit weighed almost two tons.

Other details intrigued women -- and not a few men. They included highlighting her hair blond, waxing of the legs, and maintaining her weight. The consumption of diet sodas to achieve the latter probably contributed to her depression and bulimia (Chapter 31).

The Gown

Princess Diana wore a deep pink velvet sheath with a low-dropped back, long sleeves, front slit... along with a pearl choker and drop earrings (see Front Cover and Photo Section). Backless dresses were clearly "in" as she set the trend in style.

After carefully studying the gown, Carol preferred the midnight-blue velvet dress that Diana had worn -- with matching long blue suede gloves -- to the White House dinner the previous day. Since she had conducted her own three-hour talk show (radio station WPBR) for over four years, specifically on the topic of fashion, this opinion commanded respect.

A Display of Haute Couture

Invited ladies knew two things about The Ball. First, it would be <u>very</u> formal. Second, most would have to use their imagination as to how to dress "royally" in an appropriate manner.

Secrecy abounded. Even I didn't know what my wife planned to wear as she headed for her dressmaker to pick up a gown three days before the event!

There had been a run on expensive long and colorful evening gowns. Short dresses were definitely "out."

Newspapers and television gave accounts of the gowns to be worn, along with "the source." The same interest had been shown in Washington for the White House reception. When Gloria Vanderbilt appeared on Larry King's television show, she was promptly asked about the antique dress (obtained some 30 years previously) she planned to wear.

The designer dresses worn by Palm Beachers qualified as "the social fabric."

- <u>Helen Boehm</u> would be wearing a dress made from an écru point de Venice wine-stained lace tablecloth, insured for $25,000, that had been in her family many years. It had taken 200 seamstresses more than a year to crochet it into a beige puffed-sleeved gown!
- <u>Jane Ylvisaker</u>, wife of the owner of the Palm Beach Polo and Country Club, planned to wear a strapless black- and fuchsia-colored dress of velvet and satin designed by Adam Beall.
- Before scratching The Ball from her date book (Chapter 6), <u>Mary Sanford</u>, chairperson of the gala event, indicated she would be wearing an Arnold Scaasi white satin dress with black lace over the bodice.
- <u>Rose Sachs</u> selected an off-white taffeta ball gown designed by Tita Rossi of Rome.
- The black dress worn by <u>Joan Collins</u> "had almost no front." Suzy (Aileen Mehle), the columnist, observed that she wore long, black gloves "in case anything popped out" (*Palm Beach Daily News* November 18, 1985, p. 2).
- <u>Marylou Whitney</u> had a dress designed by the Emmanuels, the British Couple who designed the Princess' wedding gown.
- <u>Tova Leidesdorf</u>, a former Miss Israel, indicated that she would don a Nina Ricci gown. It was made in Switzerland, and then flown to Paris for completion.

By contrast, a few of the invited socialites disclaimed any anxieties relative to the wardrobe they would be selecting for The Ball. Celia Lipton Farris stated: "I always leave those decisions for the last minute" (*Palm Beach Daily News* November 6, 1985, p. 1).

20

The Dinner/Ball

The doors to the Venetian Ballroom opened for The Ball after a reception in the Mediterranean Room.

Initial Impressions

Having attended numerous events in this ballroom, we could appreciate the considerable preparation involved -- especially the buffing and polishing of the huge chandeliers and marble floors.

- The dais extended along the entire east wall.
- The tables were covered with gold cloth and lace overlays.
- Masses of silk flowers with fall colors adorned each of the ballroom's four crystal chandeliers.
- The windows were secured (Chapter 18).
- The program listed patrons and benefactors, including the since-disengaged "Palm Beach Chairman" Mary Sanford.
- A beautiful -- and costly -- book honoring Dr. Hammer had been placed on the seats for women. It contained greetings to Dr. Hammer from the Prince and Princess of Wales (signed "Charles"), President Ronald Reagan (signed "Ron"), and numerous other officials.

The Guests

The following is a partial list of guests... omitting the entertainers and their spouses.

Joe Albritton, publisher and financier
Warren Avis, rental car mogul
Edmund G. Brown Sr., former Governor of California
Joan Collins, actress
Mike Curb, former Lieutenant Governor of California
Guilford Dudley, former Ambassador to Denmark
Malcolm Forbes, publisher of *Forbes* Magazine
Albert Gore Sr., former Senator from Tennessee
Eva Gabor, actress
Paula Hawkins, U.S. Senator from Florida
His Royal Highness, Prince Michael of Yugoslavia
Louis Nizer, attorney
Gregory Peck, actor
Roger Penske, auto racing businessman
H. Ross Perot, Dallas computer mogul
Abigail Van Buren Phillips (*Dear Abby*)
Laurance S. Rockefeller, philanthropist
His Majesty the Sultan of Oman, Ali Salim Bader al Hina (dressed in native attire)
Donald Trump, real estate and sports magnate
Ted Turner, media and sports mogul
Jerry Weintraub, producer
Sir Oliver Wright, British Ambassador to the United States

About two dozen Palm Beachers attended The Ball. We recognized Celia Lipton Farris, Stayton Addison, Dr. and Mrs. Henri Kayzer-Andre, the Arthur Leidesdorfs, the Howard Goodmans, Rose Sachs, Helen Boehm, Marylou Vanderbilt Whitney, and Mayor Deedy Marix with her husband Nigel. But it was strange not seeing many of the notable residents of Palm Beach who regularly attend "exclusive" parties. Some examples: Ambassador Earl E.T. Smith; Listerine heiress Sue Whitmore; Douglas Fairbanks, Jr.; Town Council President Paul Ilyinsky.

At Table No. 23, our dinner companions included two Occidental Petroleum executives, the British Consul-General from Atlanta and his wife, and a lovely female lawyer from New York. Joan Collins and her new husband sat just behind me. Former Governor and Mrs. Edmund G. Brown of California occupied another adjacent table.

At intervals, I scanned the crowd of distinguished men and beautifully dressed and coiffed women attending this world-class social spectacle. The nearby presence of Joan Collins heightened awareness of the extravaganza. One couldn't disregard the diamond barrettes in her hair, and the huge diamonds in her necklace and earrings.

Some were intrigued by an alleged "Di-nasty" wherein the Princess reportedly had blackballed this actress from a dinner at the White House because of the perception she had "upstaged" Queen Elizabeth. Collins' agent regarded the matter as a "fabrication" and "un-savory rubbish" (*Palm Beach Daily News* November 7, 1985, p. 1).

The Menu

The menu included chilled water cress soup, stuffed shells with ricotta, imported Norwegian salmon with hollandaise sauce, and coupe Diana. The wines served were Simi Chardonnay 1983, Simi Pinot Noir 1981, and Moët Brut Imperial Champagne.

This dinner definitely was not "Yuck"... a word the Princess once had used to describe dinners at Buckingham Palace. The *Palm Beach Daily News* gave detailed recipes for some items on the menu; the instructions for coupe Diana appeared in its December 8, 1985 edition.

The serving of asparagus raised several thoughts.

- Another word for asparagus tree is a crown.
- Bill Rathje, a professor at the University of Arizona whose "social research" entails sifting household trash, made this observation in another context: "With fresh asparagus, the higher your income, the higher up the stalk you cut off the tip."

Karl Ronaszeki (Executive Chef) and Bernd Lembcke (Director of Food and Beverage at The Breakers Hotel) became ecstatic when they later received word from Buckingham Palace that the Prince and Princess had been highly complimentary about the menu served (*Palm Beach Daily News* December 8, 1985, p. B-8). Indeed, Diana commented that she wouldn't be able to fit into her clothes if she stayed two more days and ate their food.

Tablehopping

Extending greetings to dignitary-friends sitting at the head table during lulls in serving dinner is an accepted practice at formal events held in The Breakers. This was definitely <u>not</u> encouraged at The Ball. Several guests, however, couldn't resist the temptation... including Ted Turner and his wife.

Speeches

After dinner, Dr. Hammer and the Prince of Wales gave stirring addresses concerning the role of the United World Colleges in fostering international peace and understanding. As far as Hammer was concerned, The Ball had been an outstanding success. Four million dollars (!) were raised for Dr. Hammer's college in New Mexico -- double the original goal. About 50 of those present had been benefactors... meaning $25,000 per ticket. *The Miami Herald* captured the success of the Ball in its eye-catcher headline: "Hammer's Bash Was a Smash for Raising Cash" (May 30, 1986, p. B-1).

Prince Charles pulled no punches in his speech about being "fed up" with "snide comments" concerning this fund-raising effort for the United World College of the American West. His use of the terms "hell" and "damn," for emphasis, went over well with the crowd. Referring to innuendos about an "elite" school, he asked: "What I want to know is what's wrong with an elite? No one complains about elite troops. How does anyone expect anything to get done unless we develop people's character as well as their minds?"

The partygoers then rendered their version of Happy Birthday to Prince Charles, who was to turn 37 the next day.

Entertainment

The audience was entertained by Victor Borge and Bob Hope (see Photo Section).

Victor Borge punned about playing a "polo-naise" and the "Hammer-klavier" sonata. As a physician used to carrying a beeper (which I <u>didn't</u> take with me that evening), I nearly went into hysterics when this entertainer interrupted his playing after someone's beeper went off. He asked: "Is there a train coming through here?"

Bob Hope began by noting that he had performed in the movies, on the stage and for television, but now ended up "entertaining a couple of tourists" in Palm Beach. He did offer some advice to the Royal Couple: "You should go into show business, where the <u>real</u> money is." Hope then fired off other jokes about royalty.

- "The Prince and Princess have replaced rock stars as England's greatest exports."
- Hope recalled his impression when performing for 18 members of the Royal Family: "watching a chess game... live."

Palm Beach itself was too juicy a morsel for Bob Hope to pass up. (Perhaps it was just as well that many of its old-time residents didn't hear several jokes of this genre.) Some samplers:

- "Palm Beachers made their money the old-fashioned way. They inherited it."
- "The radiators of the Rolls Royces in Palm Beach are filled with Perrier water."
- "Palm Beach... that's old money spelled backwards."
- "In Palm Beach, they inquire about which deck on the Mayflower."

Having attended scores of formal affairs in this ballroom, we detected another unique feature. Once the band starts playing, most couples head for the dance floor. But none dared doing so, to the tune of the Michael Carney Orchestra, until the Prince and Princess began their dance... about 11:20 PM. Once the ice had been broken, we followed suit. By this time, their Royal Highnesses were dancing with other partners. Recalling our dance alongside the Duke and Duchess of Windsor two decades previously, I remarked to Carol: "Well, now you've danced on the same floor with <u>two</u> Princes of Wales."

Neither Carol nor I danced with the Prince or Princess. Having read that John Travolta had done so with Diana the day before at the White House, this remained an unfulfilled fantasy.

It seems that Nancy Reagan approached Travolta early in the evening to relay a message: the Princess wished to dance with him. She later approached him and whispered, "It's time, John." This twosome then whirled to the theme from *Saturday Night Fever*. Travolta remarked: "She's a great little mover."

Cinderella ...again

Another touch of Cinderella ensued. Shortly after midnight, Carol reluctantly reminded me as we danced, "We'll have to leave soon. I've got a city to run, and an important meeting scheduled the first thing in the morning." Adjacent couples on the floor at the time included the Gregory Pecks, the H. Ross Perots, and Joan Collins with her new husband.

As we prepared to leave the ballroom, Mort Kaye, a Palm Beach photographer, accosted us for a picture. All the other photographers had been promptly escorted out of the chamber following the address by Prince Charles... and were not allowed to return. Even pictures taken by the invited guests were strictly verboten -- as we observed when

The Duke and Duchess of Windsor, with their pets, being greeted by Robert R. Young at the West Palm Beach Train Station. *(Courtesy of the Historical Society of Palm Beach County)*

The Duke of Windsor strolling down Worth Avenue. *(Courtesy of the Historical Society of Palm Beach County)*

Mayor Carol Roberts greeting Princess Diana at Palm Beach International Airport, as Dr. Roberts shakes the hand of Prince Charles. Armand Hammer, Chairman of Occidental Petroleum, is at the right. *(Courtesy of Davidoff Studios, Palm Beach)*

Princess Diana receiving flowers on her arrival at Palm Beach International Airport.
(Courtesy of Davidoff Studios, Palm Beach)

Prince Charles arriving at Palm Beach International Airport. *(Courtesy of Davidoff Studios, Palm Beach)*

Prince Charles playing polo at the Palm Beach Polo and Country Club. *(Courtesy of Davidoff Studios, Palm Beach)*

Mayor Carol Roberts presenting the Key to West Palm Beach on October 14, 1985 to Michael Hewitt, Her Majesty's Consul, for the Prince and Princess of Wales. *(Courtesy of Davidoff Studios, Palm Beach)*

Mayor Carol Roberts with Gregory Peck at the Norton Museum of Art. *(Courtesy of Mort Kaye Studios, Inc., Palm Beach)*

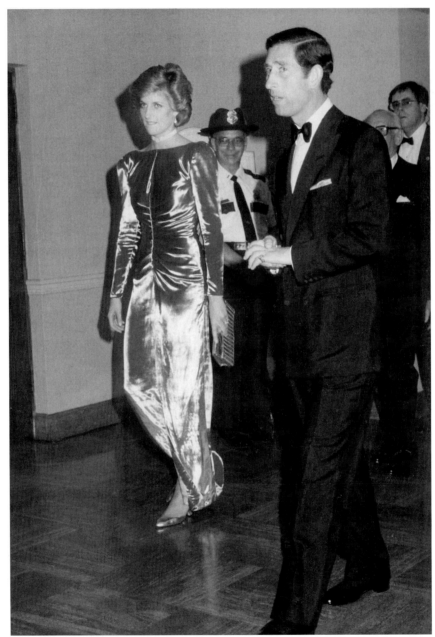

Prince Charles and Princess Diana entering the Breakers Hotel for The Ball. *(Courtesy of Davidoff Studios, Palm Beach)*

Mr. and Mrs. Ted Turner at the Breakers Hotel.
(Courtesy of Davidoff Studios, Palm Beach)

Mr. and Mrs. Victor Borge at the Breakers Hotel.
(Courtesy of Davidoff Studios, Palm Beach)

Mr. and Mrs. H. Ross Perot at the Breakers Hotel. *(Courtesy of Davidoff Studios, Palm Beach)*

Prince Philip at a fund-raiser for Outward Bound held at The Breakers Hotel on March 15, 1996. He is shown with Ann Appleman, chairperson of the gala (center), and Dina Capehart. *(Courtesy of Lucien Capehart Photography, Palm Beach)*

Visit of HRH Prince Philip in Palm Beach during March 1993.
(Courtesy of Mort Kaye Studios, Inc., Palm Beach)

HRH Prince Philip, husband of Queen Elizabeth II, arriving at the Port of Palm Beach on the yacht Britannia on March 16, 1996. *(Courtesy of Lucien Capehart Photography, Palm Beach)*

Scene from *Scooter in Palm Beach* showing Carol Roberts, playing the role of Mrs. Ratskill, entertaining royal visitors in Palm Beach. *(Courtesy of Victoria Productions)*

Former Prime Minister Margaret Thatcher meeting Palm Beach County Commissioner Carol Roberts. *(Courtesy of Mort Kaye Studios, Inc. Palm Beach)*

Lana Marks, close friend of Princess Diana, and Dr. H.J. Roberts.

Lana Marks recalling anecdote about Princess
Diana.

Robert Spencer, Second cousin of Princess Diana and a
winter resident of Palm Beach, leaving the Episcopal
Church of Bethesda-by-the-Sea after a service honoring
her memory held on September 13, 1997.

Dr. H.J. Roberts with a mourning congregant after the
Memorial Service at Episcopal Church of
Bethesda-by-the-Sea.

one woman pulled out a camera to photograph the Royal Couple dancing. But Mort knew his way around The Breakers from long experience.

Crowds were still cordoned off on the adjacent parking lot. An alert writer for the London *Mirror* detected our early departure. He trailed us and pleaded for morsels of information, such as "With whom was the Princess dancing?", and "Why are you leaving before the Royal Couple?" Concerning the latter, our briefings had not mandated that we adhere to court protocol for England.

Heading home, Carol and I kept savoring these never-to-be-forgotten two days. Our impression that this was the final curtain, however, proved wrong. Without having tried, we had become "instant celebrities" (Chapter 21), and recipients of the associated fallout.

Shortly after we departed, the Prince and Princess also decided to call it quits. They merely shook hands with some guests who lined up, and were guided out by security personnel.

Trump Connections

Another connection between Palm Beach and Princess Diana developed a decade later. Her new friend Dodi Fayed (Chapter 29) dated Marla Maples before she married Donald Trump, the owner of palatial Mar-a-Lago.

The unexpected visit of Prince Charles with Trump (Chapter 27), and the rumor about membership of the Royal Couple at his Palm Beach club (Chapter 28) will be discussed in later chapters.

Section VI

ROYAL POSTCRIPTS

Observation is more than seeing; it is knowing what you see and comprehending its significance. The process is far more mental than photographic. True observation implies studying the object and drawing conclusions from what is seen.

Charles Gow

21

Instant Celebrities

The involvement of the Roberts with this visit by Royal Couple had a lasting impact. In the eyes of the public, the very act of shaking hands with Charles and Diana conveyed a "Touch of Royalty." We were constantly teased with the same remark: "Can I touch the hand that touched royalty?"

Palm Beach Invitations

The Roberts received invitations to various functions in Palm Beach from acquaintances who lived there. Astonished, we found ourselves perceived as "in" persons by local society.

There were two notable consequences. First, our professional and personal schedules became so saturated that we had to refuse many invitations. Second, we began to covet spending more "free evenings" together... alone.

Encounters at the Theater

Opening night of *Purlie* at the Florida Repertory Theater, a black-tie affair, took place two days after The Ball.

As strong supporters of this community theatrical group, Carol and I felt obliged to attend... notwithstanding intensely active and long schedules that day. Arriving ten minutes after the performance began, we entered as unobtrusively as possible. We then stood quietly at one side of the lobby during intermission. Even so, dozens of theater-goers clasped our hands and asked the same battery of questions.

Famished by the time the play ended, we headed for a restaurant in Palm Beach that was still open, along with Scott (son #5) and another couple. Although seated in an inconspicuous corner, the other diners kept staring at us. One of our friends remarked: "They recognize you from the TV coverage of Charles and Diana."

Calls from Relatives

Relatives in other areas either saw us on television or read about our involvement with the Royal Couple in their local newspapers. Result: phone calls to "My Relatives, The Celebrities."

- A cousin-banker in Miami ended his conversation: "Now remember, Carol, you're still my cousin, whom I used to beat at Monopoly when we were kids!"
- My brother and sister-in-law rang the next Sunday morning from Boston. They had read a feature on our "royal encounter" in the November 13 issue of *The Boston Globe* titled, "Fantasy Land For A Day." Ida pleaded: "Please, tell me all about it!"

The Tuxedo Encounter

I mentioned the circumstance necessitating my purchase of a new tuxedo on the morning before The Ball (Chapter 18). But finding a suit that fit turned out to be a physical and emotional ordeal.

I arrived at the fourth West Palm Beach establishment in this search at 10 AM. The door was closed. When I knocked, a woman in the rear ducked out of sight. I then noticed a small sign indicating that the store didn't open until 10:30 AM. But it was almost time to return in order to dress for the reception at the airport. I didn't know where else to go.

As I was about to leave, a young woman got out of her car and headed for the front door.

H.J.R.: "Do you work here?"
Clerk: "Yes. Why?"
H.J.R.: "I need a new formal outfit for this evening."
Clerk: "Well, the store doesn't open until 10:30."
H.J.R.: "I just saw this sign, Miss, but I'd greatly appreciate your help in finding something that fits. I really am pressed for time."
Clerk: "Renting or buying?"
H.J.R.: "Buying."
Clerk (nonchalantly): "Well, I suppose I could look."

The next 15 minutes were hardly a display of effective salesmanship. To put it mildly, this clerk couldn't have cared less. She first flipped through several Pierre Cardin tuxedos, for which I had expressed a preference. Without even asking me to try on a coat for fit, she abruptly stated: "Nothing here in your size."

I then prevailed upon her to check other makes. She found one that was my size, and condescended when I insisted upon trying it on. It wasn't a perfect fit, but acceptable under the circumstances. The clerk then informed me that the trousers had to be purchased even though I already had three pairs. I yielded and donned them. They had to be let out.

Clerk: "How much should the waist be let out?"
H.J.R.: "I really don't know... probably about an inch."
Clerk: "How long are your legs?"
H.J.R.: "They have to be measured because there's a difference in length between the two."
Clerk: "Well, I suppose I'll just have to measure them."
H.J.R.: "Would it be possible to have the pants done today?"
Clerk: "Our fitter is here. I'll ask her."

The clerk summoned the fitter. She turned out to be the same woman who vanished from my sight when I knocked on the door. After some mumbo-jumbo, the clerk said: "O.K., pick them up by 5 PM." I wrote a check, and stated that someone would pick up the trousers.

Mrs. Helen Musgrave, my nurse, kindly agreed to perform this errand after she left the office. Her visit at this establishment headed my encounters as an "instant celebrity."

One would never have guessed the ensuing reactions of the clerk and the fitter who had been so indifferent only a few hours previously. With eyes glued to a TV set, they saw me receiving the Prince and the Princess of Wales at the airport. Mrs. Musgrave related their awed astonishment and excited questioning when she picked up the trousers. "Who is he?" "How come he was receiving them at the airport?"

Several friends offered similar versions of clerk indifference when I mentioned this story. One said: "Unfortunately, your encounter with those clerks is typical. You now know what it's like to get sales persons to wait on you these days!"

More Encounters with Clerks

Within a week after the visit by the Royal Couple, an enterprising local photographer sent me a picture of Carol greeting the Prince and Princess at the airport (see Photo Section). It was a black-and-white copy of the shot he obtained with telephoto lens.

Several days later, I went to purchase an appropriate frame for this memento at a department store I had patronized over three decades. It seemed like a rerun of my encounter in trying to purchase a tuxedo. One clerk clearly considered the selection of a frame as too trivial. I therefore had to pick one myself. The clerk remained aloof when I requested that it be wrapped. I hinted: "You might be surprised whose picture will be in it."

A delivery boy for the firm happened to be standing behind me. Out of a clear blue sky, he said: "Probably the Prince and Princess." Whirling around, I found a teenager. Congratulating him for astuteness, a revelation suddenly struck the clerk.

Physicians and Hospital Personnel

I began making rounds at the Good Samaritan Hospital on Wednesday morning... the day after The Ball. Although I tried focusing strictly on medical matters, it proved impossible. Awed physician-colleagues and nurses began bombarding me with questions that were to be repeated for weeks to come.

"Is Di really as beautiful as her pictures?"
"Is Joan Collins really as glamorous in person as on TV... for her age?"
"Can I touch the hand that shook the hands of the Prince and the Princess?"
"You must tell us all about the ball!"

As for Carol, there was no letup in such interrogation. She became hoarse from replying when we attended the annual meeting of the Palm Beach County Medical Society at which new officers were to be installed.

A Delayed Question

I had lunch with a medical colleague and two senior nurses at the Good Samaritan Hospital on April 6, 1986... five months later. As I began eating, he leaned over and asked: "Can we touch the hand that touched royalty?"

Patient Encounters

It was much the same in my office... but with more twists.

My appointment book was generally filled weeks in advance. Within days after the royal visit, dozens of patients suddenly decided that it was time for their "annual checkups" -- including some who had studiously avoided doing so for several years. Concomitantly, the expected cancellation of a few appointments became a rarity, even as Hurricane Kate made its threatening move in our direction.

My behavior remained consistent throughout. I was determined not to mention our encounters with the Royal Couple unless asked. But it didn't matter. Dozens of patients fired the same questions, coupled with a barrage of novel comments.

- I was taken aback when one patient referred to "your meeting with the POW." I then realized that the acronym for "prisoner of war" also applied to the Prince of Wales.
- Another patient sent this note: "I saw you and Carol meeting Prince Charles and Princess Di. Some people travel in the best circles."
- A Palm Beacher vented her ire to a member of my staff: "Some dumbbell blocked the view of Mrs. Roberts in that picture taken at the airport!" My secretary tactfully informed her that the "dumbbell" was none other than Prince Charles.

The psychological basis for such "annual checkups" was understandable: the opportunity for an ultimate in one-upmanship by patients who could declare: "Why, my doctor was the only member of the medical profession even allowed near Charles and Di." (Not strictly true since Armand Hammer also was a physician.)

The response of certain patients who had earned national and international distinction came as a surprise. Indeed, I had previously told several: "I consider it a great honor to be your personal physician." But our encounter with Their Royal Highnesses managed to turn things around 180 degrees.

One individual in this category was president of a household-name department store chain. Two days after the visit of the Royal Couple, he was seen for a previously-scheduled appointment, accompanied by his wife. Pleading for a first-hand account of the events, their eyes nearly popped when I described our meetings with Gregory Peck and Joan Collins.

Nearly every female patient, of course, wanted to know my gut reaction about Princess Diana. I generally replied: "She is a tall and gracious young woman." But some weren't satisfied. One asked: "Is she as glamorous and beautiful as Mrs. Roberts?" Unwilling to comment on such a sensitive and subjective matter, I invoked both personal bias and limited objectivity.

22

Correspondence

Letters from Buckingham Palace

A letter addressed to "Mr. H. J. Roberts, M.D." arrived at my office. It bore a London postmark. The only identification was an unfamiliar insignia on the back. Thinking it was yet another solicitation for inclusion in an elitist biographical compilation extracted from *Who's Who in America*, this envelope was destined for the circular file after being opened.

It became apparent that the sender assumed that the insignia would be promptly recognized as that of Buckingham Palace! Moreover, the "Mr." before my name had been intended to convey special respect.

This correspondence, dated April 10, 1986, came from David Boycroft, "Assistant Private Secretary to H.R.H. The Prince of Wales." It pertained to several of my suggestions concerning a joint effort by Rotary International and the United World Colleges (see below). The note read:

> "The Prince of Wales has asked me to thank you very much for your letter of 26th March and for the enclosures.

> "His Royal Highness was most grateful for your kind thought in writing, and has asked me to pass on his sincere thanks and best wishes."

Carol and I later received a Christmas card featuring the Royal Coat of Arms on the cover, and a view of Buckingham Palace in the center. Its "Season's Greetings" were signed by Michael Hewitt, the British Consul-General in Atlanta, and his wife Anne.

The Hammer-Roberts Letters

I reflected at length upon the speeches made by Armand Hammer and Prince Charles relative to the United World Colleges -- especially their potential for serving as viable instruments to attain peace. Being a Paul Harris Fellow of Rotary International, their remarks at the Ball had an impact. It increased while reading a feature in the October edition of *The Rotarian* about the Armand Hammer United World College of the American West.

After discussions with key persons at Rotary International, I sent this letter, dated November 21, 1985, to Dr. Hammer.

> "My wife, Mayor Carol Roberts of West Palm Beach, and I again express our appreciation to you and your colleagues for having honored our community with your recent visit.
>
> "I am enclosing a copy of the October issue of *The Rotarian* to which I referred. It contains an excellent article on the Armand Hammer United World College of the American West (pages 24-27).
>
> "I also am enclosing a copy of correspondence to Prince Charles that may be of considerable interest to you. In essence, I have asked his input relative to the possibility of some informal association between Rotary International (one million members) and the United

World Colleges. For reference, I am a founder of my Rotary club, and a Paul Harris Fellow of Rotary International.

"The enormous potential of these two organizations with the same goals working together intrigues me. I discussed this idea with several of your colleagues who were impressed by the opportunities. Needless to say, I welcome your thoughts on the matter before engaging in further discussions with Rotary International."

Unaware of the above correspondence, Armand Hammer had written us this letter, dated December 2, 1985.

"Dear Madame Mayor and Dr. Roberts:

"It meant a great deal to me to hold the exhibit opening and dinner to benefit the United World Colleges at the beautiful Norton Gallery of Art.

"I was also delighted to have you both join me and Their Royal Highnesses The Prince and Princess of Wales at the International Gala. Prince Charles expressed the goals and achievements of the United World Colleges more clearly than any spokesman I have ever heard and many scholarships are now available to deserving students.

"As a token of my appreciation, a catalog from the Armand Hammer Collection, "Five Centuries of Masterpieces," will be sent to you under separate cover.

"Thank you for your very kind hospitality."

Williams Brooks

William Brooks is General Manager of local television station WPTV. Bill and I grew up in adjacent Boston neighborhoods. We often ribbed one another about our "roots" in The Hub.

I received a package from Bill addressed to "Lord Mayor and Doctor Roberts" early in December. It contained a VCR copy of the station's coverage of the Royal Couple's arrival at the airport. The accompanying letter read: "Not bad for a little kid from Blue Hill Avenue! When the Prince celebrates his 25th anniversary as King, my hope is that you both will review this tape once again. All best wishes."

23

More On Polo

An Inside Story

Carol and I attended the Confrerie de la Chaine des Rotisseurs banquet at MacArthur's Vineyard in February 1986. A member of the Chaine seated at our table had supervised the luncheon for the Royal Couple at the Polo Club. Recalling our presence there (Chapter 16), he provided additional insights, such as removing table cards five minutes before the luncheon.

This chap, a member of the Order of the Garter, wore his medal for the luncheon. Prince Charles promptly noted it.

Prince: "What are you doing here?"
Friend: "I work here."
Prince: "How long have you done so?"
Friend: "Only a few weeks."
Prince: (making a friendly tap on the fellow's chest) "Great to meet you."

Our dinner companion could not say enough nice things about the Prince and Diana. During their stay in Wellington, she came out of her house one hot day to offer the detectives on duty a drink. An officer stated: "Water will be just fine." But the Princess thought otherwise, and brought two glasses. "I think you'd prefer water and beer, wouldn't you?"

Polo for the Masses

Local interest about sports in general led to an experiment aimed at making polo available to the average man. The National Polo League, founded by William Ylvisaker, suggested a condensed form of the ancient sport (*The Miami Herald* March 25, 1986, p. B-3).

- The field would be shortened in length from 300 to 200 yards.
- There would be three players per team, rather than the traditional four.
- Substitutes would be used as in other sports.
- The number of periods would be reduced to four (instead of six).

Zsa Zsa Gabor

Zsa Zsa Gabor connected indirectly with the Royal Couple in two ways. First, she had assumed the "Touch of Royalty" by marrying Prince Frederick von Anhalt. Second, she purchased the three-bedroom house that William Ylvisaker had given the Prince and Princess of Wales seven years previously as a wedding gift (*The Palm Beach Post* April 19, 1988, p. B-3). Gabor paid $275,000 for it -- $75,000 more than for a nearby house she had sold three years previously.

A Return Visit "On Location"

A film producer selected Carol Roberts for a lead role in the full-length movie *Scooter in Palm Beach* after scores of would-be stars flunked their screen tests. This venture had been initiated as a quasi-joke when Sandy, her brother, met the desperate producer. While signing a 14-page contract, Carol commented: "It seems I'm reversing the way Ronald Reagan did it. In my case, the politician is becoming an actor."

The film's plot had several remarkable coincidences with the theme of this book. Carol played the role of a fictitious *nouveau riche* woman living in Palm Beach who planned to entertain the Prince and Princess of Wales at a formal dinner (see Photo Section). The setting was a mansion on the island.

Another scene featured the Palm Beach Polo and Country Club. Shooting was held all day on a Sunday. Deciding to observe the action first hand, I took a detour to Wellington en route to the hospital... camera in hand for any "photo opportunities."

Finding the clubhouse where we had lunched with the Prince and Princess posed no problem. Neither did locating the action. There were numerous camera men, sound men, reflectors, other strange recording apparatus, and lots of persons "on location" seated around tables or acting as if they were waiting on them.

Hearing Carol's unmistakable laughter, I reflexively turned in her direction. There was my wife at the center of the action, carrying on and talking with several "socialites" in an affected Palm Beach accent -- just as she had pantomimed many times with our daughter Pamela about acquaintances seeking upward social mobility on the fantasy island. Indeed, anyone who didn't know differently would have sworn that Carol was a professional actress convincingly playing the role. She also offered the director suggestions for making the scene even more realistic... such as gently twirling her golden necklace during the conversation. All the while, I kept hearing members of the production team commenting "She's great!" and "That's perfect!"

Sale of The Palm Beach Polo and Country Club

Gould Inc. owned most of the property in Wellington. William Ylvisaker, chief executive officer of this electronics firm as well as an avid polo player, had purchased over 10,000 acres for development as a community and polo facility. He sold 8,650 acres in 1985, keeping the 650-acre Polo Club and about 1,100 acres of contiguous property.

The national publicity that the Polo and Country Club received as a result of the Royal Couple's visit could not have been timed better for this corporation. Faced with a net loss of more than $175 million in 1985, it decided to divest itself of nonelectronics businesses... including the Polo and Country Club. Ylvisaker told *Florida Trend* Magazine that the facility would be put up for sale when it could command a high selling price. The profit motive clearly superseded his passion for polo. A formal intent to sell the Club was announced in January 1986 (*The Evening Times* January 24, 1986, p. A-20).

Swearing Off Polo

A dramatic message later emanated from Buckingham Palace: the Prince of Wales was swearing off polo for two alleged reasons. First, the game had become more tiring and dangerous. Second, he felt obligated to devote more time to affairs of state.

It was necessary, however, to read between the lines. Had the Queen put down her royal foot because this sports "love affair" of her "idle rich" son -- along with other personal pursuits -- threatened the monarchy (Chapter 30)?

24

Armand Hammer

(continued)

The intriguing life and activities of Dr. Armand Hammer warrant more elaboration than presented in earlier chapters.

Shocking revelations surfaced about this tycoon who firmly believed that money could buy everybody and everything... an assertion made by his third wife, whose own millions had been exploited by Hammer. They derive in part from previously-secret Soviet archives confirming suspicions of his complicity in Soviet espionage. It appears that the Kremlin used Hammer's business activities as a cover for laundering money to finance its spy operations here and in Western Europe.

Greed and the Lust For Power

Edward Jay Epstein elaborated on Hammer's morbid greed, ambition and hunger for power (rather than solely for money) in *Dossier: The Secret History of Armand Hammer* (Random House). He began with this observation by Balzac: "Behind every great fortune is a crime."

> Robin Leach, best known for hosting *Lifestyles of the Rich and Famous*, offered a related observation while addressing the Palm Beach Rotary Club (October 31, 1996). Having made a career out of "champagne wishes and caviar dreams," Leach noted that the most successful persons he had interviewed were not driven primarily to obtain money, but rather to achieve success and power. This was especially impressive for individuals coming from a humble background.

Knowledgeable persons began seeking the angles for Dr. Hammer's purported philanthropy. Several will be described. Mention was made in Chapter 4 of the pardon by President George Bush for Hammer's alleged Watergate-related crimes.

The elements of greed and miserliness repeatedly became evident, as in the case of Hammer's claim against the estate of his brother (see below). Other instances involved

- The Ronald Reagan Library, which had to sue Hammer's estate for the $650,000 he pledged to that shrine.
- The $250,000 Hammer owed the National Symphony Orchestra for playing at his 90th birthday party.
- Cheating his mistresses and their children out of promised inheritances.

Hammer v. Hammer

November 13, 1985... the day after The Ball. *The Miami Herald* reported a $665,000 claim by Armand Hammer against the estate of Victor Hammer, his late brother. The suit sought reimbursement of monies that Dr. Hammer allegedly had paid to maintain his brother's gallery in New York. (Having amassed a fortune in Russian art, coupled with reproductions, the Hammer brothers founded the Hammer Gallery in New York City more than a half century previously.) The suit asked for the payment of five promissory notes signed by Victor between December 6, 1983 and April 14, 1985... plus interest from the day these notes were issued.

Victor Hammer's relatives and friends expressed great indignation. His daughter stated, "It's absolutely incredible that a person of such enormous wealth as Armand Hammer would seek to destroy his brother's family."

The reactions by Hammer's local critics were equally intense. A distinguished publisher-patient voiced criticism of such legal action. Recounting how he had rubbed elbows with Hammer at a stand in the Palm Beach Polo and Country Club, where the tycoon was buying a hot dog, my patient commented, "Since he had just come from lunch, I could only conclude that this action indicated extreme frustration."

This matter troubled me in my capacity as both a friend and prior physician of the Victor Hammers. Victor once proudly handed me a biography of Armand after we had dined together and then visited his Palm Beach apartment.

Inasmuch as I was not privy to the reasons for this suit, Carol asked me to reserve judgment. She reflected that there are occasional "friendly lawsuits" aimed at saving taxes on an estate, thereby enabling the corpus to be transmitted to a widow or heirs. (No part of the Hammer Galleries appeared as an asset of Victor's estate.) It was a perceptive insight. Retired Circuit Court Judge James R. Knott, legal administrator of Victor Hammer's estate, indicated that the suit "was a technical requirement, and objections are made to a claim in probate court" (*The Miami Herald* December 18, 1985, p. PB-3).

Armand Hammer appeared in the chamber of Palm Beach County Circuit Judge Edward Rodgers on April 21, 1986. He stated, "My brother wanted me to be his personal representative. I feel it's my duty to take care of his estate. I think I can protect my brother's interests by being executor of his estate" (*The Palm Beach Daily News* April 22, 1986, p. 1).

Hammer told the press that the negative publicity generated by this claim had caused him considerable anguish -- especially the inference that he was trying to bankrupt his brother's estate. Arthur Groman, his longstanding personal attorney, stated that Dr. Hammer would not press the case if it harmed Victor's widow in any way.

The suit by Armand Hammer then hit a major legalistic snag. Judge Rodgers indicated that Hammer had not supplied a required notice informing him the suit was filed... which would lead to dismissal of the claim. He also denied Hammer's request to be allowed to notify Judge Knott after the legal deadline passed.

The United World Colleges

Dr. Hammer expressed his devotion to the United World Colleges, beneficiaries of the visit by himself and the Royal Couple (Chapter 1 and 20). This network (begun in 1962) included the facility in Montezuma, New Mexico. These schools were held out as a nonpolitical brainchild of Hammer aimed at advancing peace and international understanding through educating students about the horrors of war. Prince Charles led the organization after the death of Lord Mountbatten, the prior president, from a terrorist bomb.

In years to come, it became evident that Hammer's enormous ego played as great a role in this expensive venture as altruism. He allegedly spent about $5 million to finance this and other pet projects of Charles in order to procure the Prince as a royal sponsor for the Nobel Peace Prize! Hammer courted members of the Nobel committee, and even sent his art collection (see below) to Sweden. Prime Minister Menachem Begin of Israel, a previous Nobel laureate, ultimately nominated Hammer for the award during 1989 after he had offered $100 million in investments to bolster the Israeli economy. (The Dalai Lama won when there were two candidates -- he and Hammer.)

The Hammer Art Collection

The Hammer collection, *Five Centuries of Masterpieces*, remains one of the great private collections of art in the world. Its extraordinary contents were described in Chapter 10.

Here again, the prime motivation in spending a fortune to acquire these gems (largely from Occidental Petroleum Company funds) involved Hammer's overwhelming desire for respectability as well as power. The industrialist openly referred to them as his "ticket to immortality."

This attitude is further illustrated by Hammer's pressure on the directors of Occidental to purchase the Leicaster Codex -- the 470-year-old notebook of Leonardo da Vinci -- for more than $2 million in 1980. Three items demonstrate the Hammer personality.

- He renamed the work as the Codex Hammer.
- Leonardo's home town of Vinci was successfully approached to make Hammer an honorary citizen -- thereby

becoming Armand Hammer da Vinci.

- This unique manuscript was cut into separate pages to enable display of the treasure in a more theatrical manner.

More on the Codex

Leonardo wrote this notebook between 1506 and 1508 while in his fifties. It provides fascinating glimpses into the mind of an acknowledged genius whose immortal accomplishments encompassed art, science and invention at a period in the Renaissance when gifted persons attempted to link these disciplines.

Many regard the Codex as the most important of Leonardo's 21 notebooks. He sought to codify general principles and theories involving such realms as hydraulics, the "color of the air," the presence of fossils, and secondary light of the moon.

The work was previously known as the Codex Leicester because the family of the Earl of Leicester had owned it for more than two centuries. Microsoft chairman Bill Gates purchased it for $30.8 million in 1994 (the highest price ever paid for a manuscript at auction), and used the original designation. He subsequently lent this "Book of Gates" for an exhibit at New York's American Museum of National History -- each of the 18 double-sided sheets now sandwiched in glass, and placed in a separate case.

Other Hammer Vignettes

"Yes"... Finally

At long last! Dr. Hammer could respond "Yes" on being asked the same question: "Do you own Arm & Hammer, the baking soda product?" His company formed a partnership with Church & Dwight Company, Inc. However, an Occidental Petroleum spokesperson insisted that any connection with Hammer's name was purely coincidental.

A Delayed Bar Mitzvah

Armand Hammer became the focus of another swank ceremony at the age of 92. It was the occasion of his seventh bar mitzvah... 79 years after turning 13.

The billionaire celebrated this occasion in the company of many Hollywood celebrities. They included Bob Hope, Merv Griffin, Ted Turner, Elliot Gould and California Governor-elect Pete Wilson (*The Miami Herald* December 1, 1990, p. A-1).

Another fact emerged after Hammer's death that reinforced his knack for covering all the bases. He had apparently accepted Jesus on his deathbed!

A Life Shortchanged By Eight Years

This entrepreneur, physician, art collector, kingmaker, globe-trotting diplomat, corporate chieftain and philanthropist with the Midas touch died at the age of 92 from extensive cancer. His wife of 33 years had passed away the previous year, just before contemplating divorce.

Hammer's endurance proved remarkable. Even the need for a pacemaker at 91 hardly slowed his pace. Hammer's employment agreement with Occidental Petroleum Corporation reflected confidence in his longevity -- namely, it did not expire until 1998 when he would have attained the age of 100 (*The Palm Beach Post* December 11, 1990, A-1)!

Sam Walton, once considered the richest man in the United States, provided a unique perspective concerning persons who felt they had "arrived" as a result of amassing great wealth and many possessions. He soberly reflected that such individuals already were on "the return trip."

Another startling revelation followed. Hammer's estate was valued at about $40 million... not in the widely assumed billions. This again proved his genius in using "other people's money" -- including two of his wealthy wives, and Occidental Petroleum shareholders.

25

A Potpourri Of Political Fallouts

The visit of the Royal Couple, combined with that of Dr. Armand Hammer, inevitably generated political controversy. The following vignettes supplement others described in previous chapters.

Dinner for Two: The Declaration

Mayor Carol Roberts became perplexed as she filled out the form detailing "contributions and gifts" that is required of Florida's elected officials. Her confusion centered about the description and actual value of our invitation to The Ball. Was it the basic cost of dinner for two at The Breakers -- about $100 per person? Or should it reflect the amount sponsors had contributed to the United World College of the West... at least $5,000 per person?

Carol decided to take no chances, lest the document be misunderstood or become the focus of a sensationalist feature by the press. She therefore listed both amounts.

Color It Red

There were repeated references to Dr. Hammer's communist sympathies (Chapter 4 and 24). But who would have thought that the red gown worn by Princess Diana (see Front Cover) would evoke political overtones of this genre? Such a scenario became the case, however, when some locals regarded it as further proof of Hammer's Soviet connection.

Advice to Politicians

Kenneth Cuthbertson wrote an insightful note to *Time* Magazine (December 2, 1985, p. 5). He described the ability of the Royal Couple to take its role representing Britain so seriously "without taking themselves too seriously." Cuthbertson expressed the hope that "our politicians could do as much."

Voting for "Royalty"

President and Mrs. John F. Kennedy came about as close to perceived "royalty" as any American leader since George Washington. Indeed, many citizens still equate "Camelot" more with their Kennedy White House than the alleged site of King Arthur's palace and court.

Several weeks after the Prince and Princess left our shores, a "third generation" member of the Kennedy clan announced his candidacy for the seat in the House of Representatives being vacated by "Tip" O'Neill. This created an enormous challenge for those elected officials in Massachusetts who had thrown their hats into this particular ring. Most asked the basic question: "The public follows royalty. But will it vote for royalty?" It did.

There have been numerous researches into the British lineage of American presidents and those seeking the Presidency. Most recently, genealogists reported that President Bill Clinton and Republican candidate Bob Dole were distant cousins whose ancestry can be traced to King Henry III -- as well as Presidents William Henry Harrison and Benjamin Harrison. Clinton had the edge on "blue genes," however, because of his direct descent from King Robert I of France, and by virtue of a relation to every Scottish monarch. For good measure, he also was related on his mother's side to President Andrew Jackson, Davy Crockett, and Simon de Montford, Earl of Leicester (Chapter 24). (*Burke's Peerage* interjected a disconcerting assertion: Clinton's "illegitimate" descent from Henry III.)

Analysis by Buchwald

Art Buchwald, the humorous columnist, offered some perceptive comments on CNN's *Crossfire* several weeks after the Royal Couple departed.

- Art interpreted Princess Diana's visit as "the end of the sexual revolution."
- Buchwald explained his failure to attend the White House dinner held in honor of the Prince and Princess: refusal to break up a weekly poker game.
- He conjectured that politicians were beginning to outshine movie stars as America's "royalty."

26

More Postscripts

Seeking Inside Information

The Roberts continued to be bombarded with the same request: "You must tell me about Diana" (Chapter 21). Our response became virtually automatic: "She tends to be somewhat shy in crowds, but immediately relaxes and becomes animated with children. Also, both Diana and the Prince have good handshakes."

Life on Palm Beach

The *Palm Beach Daily News* headlined its edition the morning after The Ball: "British Invasion Captures P.B." Agnes Ash, editor of "The Shiny Sheet," had predicted the previous day that life would normalize for inhabitants of this community "who don't want the world intruding on this peaceful, rigidly mannered way of life" (November 12, 1985, p. B-1). She was right... but with a few reservations.

In this vein, *The Washington Post* purportedly issued this memo to Pat Kluge (Chapter 7): "You can come home now" (*The Miami Herald* November 25, 1985, p. C-1).

E Pluribus Unum

From our vantage point, the most impressive invited guest had been Gregory Peck. Other guests and gawkers at both the Norton reception and The Breakers event seemed to concur.

A picture of Carol and Gregory Peck (see Photo Section) appeared on the front page of *The Condo News* (November 20, 1985). The caption read: "The Stars Were Out." It had an enormous impact on readers. One worker at City Hall relayed a copy to Her Honor with this note, "Mayor Roberts -- You look great! And so does Greg."

Visit by Nature

Society and Nature share a common attribute: each abhors a vacuum.

This strange analogy occurred to me several days after the departure of Their Royal Highnesses when a rare November hurricane aimed at South Florida. "Kate" packed sustained winds of 110 mph, and gusts up to 126 mph. Her high winds and pounding waves affected construction workers getting ready to pour concrete for a new sea wall at the Palm Beach oceanfront home of Mollie Wilmot (of Mercedes I fame). They understandably decided to delay this project for several days.

Princes Charles and Princess Diana were fortunate in one related respect. The initial letters of the alphabet -- especially "C" and "D" -- already had been used to name prior hurricanes for that season.

"Andrew"
Subsequent meteorological events would focus on the name of another member of the royal family: Andrew. It is derived from a Greek word meaning manly.

The National Oceanic and Atmospheric Administration announced that the name of the first tropical storm or hurricane to hit the Atlantic, Caribbean or Gulf of Mexico during the 1986 hurricane season would be designated Andrew. (The names for these storms are supplied by the World Meteorological Organization in Geneva.)

Little attention was paid to the name that year. But it would later go down in history as the worst hurricane to strike South Florida. The economic toll of Hurricane Andrew's devastation on August 24, 1992 exceeded $60 billion.

Local cartoonists had a field day when Prince Andrew subsequently visited the area (Chapter 27).

Distribution of the Royal Flowers

Mention was made of the beautiful flowers the Royal Couple received on their arrival, and of others that adorned the Venetian Ballroom. At the request of the British Consul, Mayor Roberts arranged for their distribution to a large nursing home.

The director of this facility expressed gratitude for such a thoughtful and appreciated gesture in a letter published by *The Palm Beach Post* (December 13, 1985, p. A-24).

> "However, other facets of the visit were not publicized. I would like to take the opportunity to tell all of one gesture by the royal couple. They donated their flowers to either a hospital or nursing home, and Darcy Hall Nursing Home was the honored recipient of their gift."

Another Princess

One firm was not the least unhappy over "the-Princess-this, the-Princess-that" complaints by some Palm Beachers. Within two weeks, local television and radio stations began running an ad for a cruise ship that departed from the Port of Palm Beach. Its message: "A new Princess is coming to town: The Viking Princess. And she parties from morning to night."

A Sigh of Relief by the Media

Members of the local news media breathed a sigh of relief once they had completed their features about the visit by the Royal Couple. As Thanksgiving Day approached, the manager of Channel 12 gave thanks "that the Prince and Princess didn't buy a mansion in Palm Beach... otherwise we in the media would never get anything else done."

Another Cinderella Refrain

I mentioned refrains about "Cinderella" as Carol departed for The Ball, and returned at midnight.

This theme reared itself several days later in a way that had apparently escaped the Madison Avenue firm doing PR for Ayerst, the pharmaceutical company. A rib-tickling thought nearly convulsed me as I read a promotional blurb for Inderal-LA®: "If the prefix "C" -- for Cinderella -- had been inserted, this 'magic bullet' could be identified as "C-Inderal-LA."

On Seeing Reruns

Carol Roberts has never been a television addict. This includes reluctance to watch reruns of her own activities. Faced with tight schedules, she found little of interest on the boob tube other than news programs and C-SPAN features or commentaries. A comment by Alex Dreyfoos, owner of Channel 12, could have been mouthed by her: "I don't spend much time watching television. I guess (it is because) I find the things I am involved in so interesting" (*The Miami Herald* December 2, 1985, p. C-1.)

Hairdresser Perks

Something in the December 1, 1985 edition of *Parade* Magazine obviously intrigued Carol, causing her to ask: "Do you know that Nancy Reagan is accompanied by her hairdresser on diplomatic trips abroad?" The Mayor then reflected: "I guess we taxpayers also have to pay for her hairdresser."

Taxpayers both here and abroad should have welcomed two related items in this category after having viewed Princess Diana's entourage. First Prime Minister Margaret Thatcher apparently traveled only with her electric hair curlers. Second, Mayor Carol Roberts also was her own "hairdresser."

Criticism of Etiquette

The Palm Beach Post published a letter on December 2, 1985 (p. A-10) from Pipe-Major Walter T. Wilkie, D.M., Second Battalion Scot Guards. For five years, Wilkie had been the personal piper to Her Majesty Queen Elizabeth at Buckingham Palace. Having witnessed the reaction of guests attending social and state functions in England and throughout the world, he conveyed these sentiments:

> "Not so in West Palm Beach. According to the news media, circus maximus hit town. Reading of the escapades of the local social register led me to believe that the 'upper class,' excuse me while I laugh, have much to learn in the art of royal etiquette. They remind me of the queen's corgis, fighting over scraps thrown from the royal banquet table.
>
> "I am sure that His Royal Highness Prince Charles and Princess Diana laughed their way across the Atlantic, as they reminisced at the antics of the 'upper crust' of Palm Beach.
>
> "And you wonder why this country is still referred to as 'the Colonies'."[1]

[1]©1985 *The Palm Beach Post*. Reproduced with permission.

27

Subsequent Visits by Members of the Royal Family

S outh Florida -- Palm Beach in particular -- attracted the attention of members of the House of Windsor following the successful visit of the Prince and Princess of Wales. This was evidenced by their ensuing trips. Much of the excitement evaporated, however, when Charles and Diana separated and did not return as a duo. A few of these royal excursions locally and to other American cities will be recounted.

Prince Charles

Reference to the earlier visits by Prince Charles -- #1 in 1970 (Chapter 14), and #2 in 1980 (Chapter 12) -- was made in prior sections.

Other educational institutions were impressed by Dr. Hammer's PR coup. Five days after Charles' visit, the director of Harvard University's News Office issued a statement that His Royal Highness might return in the fall to help celebrate the University's 350th Anniversary. The link? The Prince of Wales graduated from Cambridge University, where founder John Harvard received an education.

Visit #4

Prince Charles returned on February 17, 1986 to Austin, Texas. He was welcomed by the sounds of bagpipes playing *The Yellow Rose of Texas* as the State began its sesquicentennial celebration of independence from Mexico.

The Prince of Wales was actually a drawing card to promote British trade. As part of the activities he attended a black-tie dinner at which he presented the Winston Churchill Foundation award to H. Ross Perot.

There was another memorable event. Charles cut a colossal birthday cake that weighted 90,000 pounds and could serve 300,000 persons! It required more than 31,000 boxes of Duncan Hines Deluxe Yellow Cake Mix and 93,000 whole eggs. This concoction took 32 hours for 163 persons to assemble. The Prince performed the feat with an 8-pound replica of the saber used by Sam Houston during the fight for independence.

Visit #5

Prince Charles returned to the Palm Beaches in March 1988... sans Diana. He was the guest of Jori and Geoffrey Kent at their Palm Beach Polo and Country Club home. This visit included attending a benefit luncheon for the Friends of the Masai Mara sponsored by Rolex, and by Abercrombie and Kent. The Prince would also play in the Rolex Challenge Cup game as part of the Windsor Park Polo team following the luncheon. It was made <u>very</u> clear to all, however, that Charles did not plan to indulge in other social activities.

The Kents founded Friends of the Masai Mara in order to preserve animals on Kenya's Masai Mara Game Reserve. Kent, a 45-year-old former British Army offer, had transformed a small family safari business in Kenya into a highly successful independent travel company. The Kents amassed a large collection of sculptures and artifacts from their travels.

The Roberts greeted Prince Charles at the airport. He arrived with deposed King Constantine of Greece. Carol's initial impression was that his "secretary" exhibited a striking improvement in his selection of a suit. When the Prince then introduced his companion as "His Royal Highness," Carol realized that her misperception reflected good taste in judging clothes. Charles was also accompanied by his press secretary, doctor, valet and personal secretary.

> Mayor Deedy Marix of Palm Beach and her husband Nigel, both former Brits, had been in the receiving line for the Royal Couple several years previously. But only Nigel was present at the Butler Aviation Executive Terminal on this occasion. He explained that Deedy was in bed with influenza. I had absolutely no reason to doubt the matter because nothing short of having one foot in the hospital could have kept her away.

Carol handed the Prince a gift-wrapped souvenir of his visit on again welcoming him -- this time as Chair of the Palm Beach County Commission. She told the press that the package contained four gold-rimmed coasters, each bearing the crest of the County. Charles then carried her gift to the maroon and tan Rolls Royce in which he was whisked to Mar-a-Lago.

> Carol's repeat performance recalled the duties of a previous West Palm Beach Mayor, Percy I. Hopkins Jr. During his two-year stint in this capacity, Hopkins greeted President John F. Kennedy whenever he visited Palm Beach (*The Palm Beach Post* January 16, 1997, p. B-4).

This unscheduled visit to Palm Beach for 50 minutes came as a surprise to Donald Trump. He was playing golf that Saturday afternoon when he learned that the Prince wished to see him and tour <u>his</u> palace (*The Miami Herald* March 6, 1988, p. A-1).

> A handful of rich and influential persons was meeting with Trump. They included John Kluge (often described as the second richest man in the United States), Tony O'Reilly (chairman of H. J. Heinz & Co.), Ann Getty (publisher and wife of another of the country's richest men), and Alexander Papamarkou (New York investment banker).

The Prince was provided a "360-degree blanket of protection" by a variety of local, state and federal agencies that had him surrounded in a "diamond-shape" net 24 hours a day.

The friendly battle between Marylou Whitney and Anna Cronholm in bidding for an Abercrombie & Kent Hemingway safari became a highlight of the auction benefitting the Kenyan game reserve. Whitney won... but it cost her $22,000. All told, this event raised $150,000 from ticket sales and the auction, which also included wildlife paintings and sculptures.

This visit made the front page of *The Palm Beach Post* (March 6, 1988, p. A-1). The same page featured a major political effort by Palm Beach County Chair Carol Roberts, who had proposed a countywide health care taxing district to improve the trauma health care system (Chapter 31).

> Prince Charles also shared the March 6, 1988 front page of the *Palm Beach Daily News* with brother Prince Andrew and his wife, the former Sarah Ferguson. The Duke and Duchess of York were visiting Southern California where they cheered the Royal Guards Polo Team.

All hands came to the same conclusion after this visit: "It was really Diana who drew the crowds."

Visit #6

Charles returned on February 18, 1989 for a weekend of polo. A virtual army of federal and local security guards monitored his activity out of concern for a possible attack by the Irish Republic Army. Accordingly, the British Embassy in Washington kept mum about details of his itinerary.

Visit #7

The Prince visited Williamsburg, Virginia, in February 1993 to help celebrate the 300th birthday of the College of William and Mary. He was aware of an ironic twist involving the nation's second oldest college. Several years previously, he confided to students that the 1677 marriage of these future monarchs had been a "bad and depressing affair" (*The New York Times* February 14, 1993, p. 16).

Visit #8

The newly-single Prince of Wales (Chapter 28) attended a benefit for the American Friends of the Black Rose (King Henry VIII's favorite warship) in Newport on July 18, 1996. Although 500 paid responses -- at $500 per person -- were expected, only 225 chose to hobnob with this ex-husband of the world's most famous single mother. Barton Gubelmann, a prominent member of Palm Beach and Newport societies, declined the invitation. He stated, "Now, if Diana were coming, that would be different" (*Palm Beach Daily News* July 18, 1996, p. 1.

Visit #3

The return of Princess Diana to Washington, D.C. in October 1990 proved a disappointment -- compared to her triumphant visits in 1985 and 1989. She had agreed to attend a fund-raising dinner for the London City Ballet, the Washington Ballet, and Grandma's House (a Washington home for children with AIDS).

It was not Diana's fault, however. The blame rested in over-ambitious organizers who set the price for individual attendance at $2,500-$3,500. The result: only 260 of the 500 regal chairs flown from London were warmed (*People* Magazine October 22, 1990). This tab proved daunting for Washington's well-heeled, who considered even $1,500 a steep price.

Visit #4

Diana revisited Washington in October 1994 as the guest of honor at a dinner hosted by Katherine Graham, publisher of *The Washington Post*.

Visit #5

Diana toured Chicago during June 1996 to raise money for cancer research.

Visit #6

Diana -- now no longer "Her Royal Highness" (Chapter 28) -- attended a fund-raiser for breast cancer research at the National Museum in Washington as honorary chairwoman. Photos showed her at a September 25, 1996 breakfast with Hillary Clinton, Ralph Lauren and Katherine Graham.

The Queen

A famous line by Queen Elizabeth II could be applied to her visits at home and abroad: "I have to be seen to be believed."

Buckingham Palace closely scrutinized the visit of the Royal Couple to the United States. Within two weeks, there was discussion about a visit in May by none other than Her Majesty. For most Americans, it probably would be as close to the Mother Goose rhyme about going to London to visit the Queen as they would ever come.

Reading this announcement, I hoped that the Queen wouldn't be disappointed by the reception. Unlike her superstar daughter-in-law, Her Royal Highness seemed to have difficulty smiling naturally. "Freezing" in the presence of photographers caused her to appear rather severe and without a sense of humor, even though she allegedly exhibited much humor in private.

Background

The formal name of Queen Elizabeth II is "Elizabeth Alexandra Mary Windsor, Queen Elizabeth the Second, by the grace of God, of the United Kingdom of Great Britain and Northern Ireland and of her other realms and Territories, Queen, Head of the Commonwealth, Defender of the Faith." She was the 42nd Monarch in Britain since William the Conqueror in 1066. In point of fact, she could trace her ancestry to Egbert, the Saxon King, in the year 829.

No one could doubt Queen Elizabeth's knowledge of government. She had studied *The English Constitution*, written by Walter Bagehot 128 years ago, at an early age. It contains this significant statement: "The sovereign has, under a constitutional monarchy such as ours, three rights -- the right to be consulted, the right to encourage, the right to warn. And a king of great sense and sagacity would want no others." Indeed, if none of the three parties -- Labor, the Conservatives, and the alliance of Liberals and Social Democrats -- won an election convincingly, the Queen would decide which party leader ought to be invited to form a government.

Queen Elizabeth had reached retirement age with a remarkable achievement... never having paid taxes despite her alleged status as the richest woman of the world. She was worth an estimated $1.7 billion!

Security for Queen Elizabeth at home and abroad had to be extensive. During a visit to Auckland, New Zealand, one protester hit her with an egg.

The Queen wore gloves because of extreme health consciousness, even on the hottest day in Africa. She also brought her own brand of drinking water (Malvern).

The Queen's 5,800-ton yacht, Britannia (see below and Photo Section), is probably the largest private yacht in the world. The vessel, part of the Royal Navy, is manned by 21 officers and 250 sailors -- referred to as "snotty yachties" throughout the senior service. They wear special rubber-soled shoes in order to minimize disturbing noises. There is a place for 56 guests around the dining room table. The dining room set features real Chippendale. Its hold stores a special Rolls Royce owned by the Queen. (The annual cost of $15.3 million to run the ship is no longer a priority budget item, and accounts for its slated leave of the fleet in late 1997.)

The Queen also has her special squadron of aircraft, known as the Queen's Flight, and a Royal Train.

The Kentucky Visit

Queen Elizabeth went to Lexington, Kentucky, on May 22, 1986 for a strictly private visit with Will and Sarah Farrish, owners of Lane's Inn Farm in Versailles, Kentucky (*Palm Beach Daily News* May 22, 1986, p. 1). She had a special passion for breeding and racing horses as part of the "royal sport." No press coverage was allowed.

An interesting Palm Beach connection surfaced during this visit. The Queen was served on green porcelain known as Dodie Thayer Lettuceware. The settings were made by Dodie Thayer, a resident of Jupiter, and obtained through Isabel Ireland, owner of Isabel's Et Cetra on County Road in Palm Beach. Isabel once stated: "We could put a sign on our door saying we service the Queen of England, but we don't."

The Miami Visit

Queen Elizabeth decided to visit Miami in May 1991. She arrive by Concorde on May 17. Her itinerary included visiting the Booker T. Washington Middle School, and Vizcaya for a reception hosted by the City of Miami and Dade County. She would then entertain guests at a formal dinner aboard the 412-foot yacht Britannia (see above), which had docked on May 10. The Queen was accompanied by her husband, Prince Philip, the Duke of Edinburgh, and a staff of 35 persons.

> For those interested in royal trivia, the Queen's entourage included her private secretary and deputy private secretary, Mistress of the Robes, Lady of the Bedchamber, Master of the Royal Household, Queen's equerry, dresser, two assistant dressers, two maids, Queen's page, footman, Page of the Presence, hairdresser, Traveling Yeoman, seven female clerks of court officials, royal chef, three senior cooks, pastry sous chef, deputy sergeant footman, three footmen, two dining room assistants, kitchen porter, three security men from Scotland Yard, Prince Philip's orderly, and two valets.

Miami was clearly impressed by this Touch of Royalty on "a regal day of white gloves, red carpets and blue blood" (*The Miami Herald* May 18, 1991, p. A-1).

- Governor Lawton Chiles greeted the Queen. He stated: "Your Majesty, we're happy to have you in Florida."
- *The Miami Herald* headlined the event as "Our Queen for a day."
- The warm spot for this Monarch crystallized in the assertion: "We quit the Empire, but still love the Queen."

The Queen subsequently set sail for the Keys, and then Tampa to meet General Norman Schwarzkopf on whom she bestowed an honorary knighthood.

There was one glaring deficiency in her itinerary to Florida: no excursion to Palm Beach.

Prince Philip

Prince Philip, the 71-year-old husband of Queen Elizabeth II, made an appearance in Palm Beach on March 24, 1993 (see Photo Section). He was to address a "distinguished influential audience at The Society of Four Arts" *Palm Beach Daily News* March 25, 1993, p. 1).

Philip arrived on the royal yacht Britannia, which docked at the Port of Palm Beach. He sported a loud blue and white Hawaiian shirt while standing on the deck. His youngest son, Prince Edward, arrived shortly thereafter at the Palm Beach International Airport to accompany his father.

The Prince spoke as international president of the Worldwide Fund for Nature. This organization had spent about $200 million on practical conservation projects during the previous year. Philip punctuated his talk with snatches of poetry, slides of art work, and renderings of birds.

Philip and his son subsequently attended a gala at the Breakers Hotel, following which they returned to the royal yacht. A pre-gala cocktail reception, sponsored by an Edinburgh distiller of Scotch whiskey, was held aboard the yacht. It was made crystal clear that neither this event nor the ship would be open to the public!

Philip was not immune to barbs from the press either at home or abroad.

- He was criticized in England for cruising around the world in a yacht that cost British taxpayers more than $15 million annually.
- His salary -- $547,000 annually for being the Duke of Edinburgh and the Royal Consort -- also evoked concern.
- The Prince raised eyebrows during his luncheon address when he compared killing for sport to butchering animals for food. He stated: "I don't think it (killing animals) for money makes it any more moral. I don't think a prostitute is more moral than a wife, but they are doing the same thing" (*The Palm Beach Post* March 24, 1993 p. B-1).
- One local columnist was banished from his 3 PM lecture at the Society of the Four Arts. The reporter later claimed the Palm Beach Dis-Invitation Stress Syndrome (*The Palm Beach Post* March 25, 1993, p. A-13).

The Palm Beach Daily News subsequently announced that Prince Philip and Prince Edward were planning to attend a fund-raising reception for Outward Bound at The Breakers on March 15, 1996 (see Photo Section). It raised one million dollars. Asked if hostesses on the island were jockeying for a chance to entertain these royal visitors, Ann Appleman, chairwoman of the event, replied: "This is Palm Beach. What do *you* think?"

The Prince stayed aboard the Britannia, which also served as a conference center for British trade groups.

The pre-gala events were hosted by Celia Lipton Farris and Barbara Wainscott. The Farris cocktail reception and the Wainscott luncheon became matters of national security (*Palm Beach Daily News* March 10, 1996, p. A-11). The former was held at Farris' historic house on El Vedado Road... once the home of Consuelo Vanderbilt Balsam. Wainscott's luncheon at her Jungle Road home for fellows of the Duke of Edinburgh's Award World Fellowship reportedly raising $75,000.

Princess Margaret

The striking differences between Queen Elizabeth II and Princess Margaret have been described by Anne Edwards in *Royal Sisters: Queen Elizabeth II and Princess Margaret* (published by William Morrow). Whereas "Lilibet" was cultivated as a possible future monarch, Margaret enjoyed the freedom to be spontaneous -- and even outrageous -- in her behavior. But tragedy had affected her personal life.

> The British public was saddened over the death, in exile, of Group Captain Peter Townsend during June 1995. Townsend had shot down eleven enemy planes and won the Distinguished Service Order, as well as two Distinguished Flying Crosses, for gallantry. Princess Margaret, who decided in 1955 not to marry him because of the establishment's disapproval of a previous divorce, experienced grief. In his 1978 autobiography, Townsend stated: "She could have married me only if she had been prepared to give up everything -- her position, her prestige, her privy purse."

Her Royal Highness The Princess Margaret, Countess of Snowdon, visited the United States a year after the Royal Couple. She came to New York City in February 1986 for a gala benefit at the Brooklyn Academy of Music by the Sadler's Wells Royal Ballet (a favorite charity of the Princess), and for a spectacular exhibit of Old Master paintings from the Dulwich Picture Gallery. The ballet company gave a gala production of *The Sleeping Beauty* for 520 influential guests.

Princess Margaret subsequently visited Palm Beach on March 8, 1989 as the guest of honor for a dinner/dance at the Beach Club. Viscountess Mary Rothermere, a Palm Beach resident, chaired this event benefitting the Sadler's Wells Ballet Company. She served on its board of directors. (Her deceased husband had been a British media baron and member of the British House of Commons.)

Only a few friends knew of this Palm Beach visit. She had driven from Hobe Sound with her hostess Dreu Heinz. Margaret then lunched with Princess Maria Pia de Savoye, oldest daughter of late King Umberto of Italy, at her home on North Lake Way (*Palm Beach Daily News* February 7, 1987, p. 1). Others in attendance at the poolside gathering included Douglas Fairbanks, Christina de Caraman Goldsmith, Prince Michael de Bourbon-Parme, and the sons of Princess Maria Pia (Prince Serge and Prince Michael of Yugoslavia).

Princess Anne

There were some misgivings about a planned visit by Princess Anne, previously dubbed by an unsympathetic British press as "Her Royal Haughtiness." It was hoped that the seeming change in both her image and attitude would influence members of the American press.

The Duchess of York

Her Royal Highness, the Duchess of York, arrived in our area on January 16, 1992 for dinner, lunch and polo. *The Palm Beach Post* headlined the visit of the former Sarah Ferguson: "The Duchess Comes To Town: Some Brits May Be Cool To Her, But We Love Her. Here's Your Chance To See The Fun-Loving Fergie" (January 16, 1992, p. D-1).

Sarah married Prince Andrew, the second son of Queen Elizabeth II, in 1986. Several Palm Beachers attended the wedding, including Celia Lipton Farris and Estee Lauder.

Americans generally responded positively to Fergie's good humor and bubbly personality. The situation contrasted with that in Britain where she got little respect from Fleet Street. Most persons on this side of the Atlantic seemed less concerned with "the girl with the past" having previous live-in relationships, who then tamed "Randy Andy." (One British columnist described the headstrong duchess as "a big yawn," and "a photo opportunity.")

Many Americans were impressed by her successful shedding of a Rubenesque figure. In fact, tabloids in both Britain and the United States ceased referring to her as the Duchess of Pork when she lost 35 pounds!

The visit of "Fergie" included a public appearance at the Palm Beach Polo and Country Club, visits to a hospital, an AIDS nursery and an emergency shelter for abused children, and dinner at several private clubs in Palm Beach. She stayed in the secluded three-bedroom beach house at 974 South Ocean Boulevard owned by Bob and Lewis Fomon, and designed by John Volk, the noted Palm Beach architect. This ocean- to-lake property, named Palmare, with 3 acres and a private tunnel to the beach, later went on the market for $8.5 million (*Palm Beach Daily News* November 3, 1995, p. 1).

The mother of the Duchess, Susan Barrantes, had a home in Wellington. She fell in love with Hector Barrantes, an Argentinean polo player and businessman, and subsequently divorced Ronald Ferguson in 1974. Fergie was 14 at the time of the divorce. Her mother first learned of Sarah's engagement to Prince Andrew during a stay at the Palm Beach Polo and Country Club.

"Fergie" subsequently signed on with the modeling agency Next Management. She also contracted with Simon & Schuster to write her autobiography for a reported $1.3 million (*Time* June 17, 1996, p. 103).

Prince Edward

H.R.H. Prince Edward Anthony Richard Louis came to Palm Beach in 1993 (see above). He returned in March 1997 for a "strictly private and personal visit" (*Palm Beach Daily News* March 5, 1997, p. 1), followed several months later for golfing at Frenchman's Creek and then the PGA National (*The Palm Beach Post* May 21, 1997, p. D-1). This 33-year-old soft-spoken and artistic Windsor -- seventh in the line of succession -- had maintained a relatively scandal-free career... unlike his older brothers and sister.

The Prince was honored at a dinner party hosted by David Berger and Barbara Wainscott at their Palm Beach home ("Elephant Walk"). The occasion also celebrated Wainscott's Big Five-Oh birthday.

The nature of this "personal visit" was not revealed. It had been noted, however, that one of his friends, Sophie Rhys Jones, underwent some "royal training" to prevent "another Fergie or Di" situation (*The Miami Herald* May 31, 1996, p. A-2).

28

Problems of a Royal Family

Only fortunetellers, Marxists and Jehovah's Witnesses will venture to prognosticate whether Prince Charles and Lady Diana will actually one day mount the throne as King and Queen of England... Popularity, however seemingly strong and widespread, can evaporate in an afternoon, and institutions that have lasted for centuries disappear overnight.

Malcolm Muggeridge
(August 3, 1981)

The House of Windsor became increasingly "Dallas-ized" after the visit by the Royal Couple. Some sympathized with the efforts of Queen Elizabeth II to control a "dysfunctional" family, especially as tabloids kept publishing exposés about Prince Charles and Princess Diana. In effect, the media had converted the fairy-tale courtship and marriage into an ongoing soap opera. The papers and television network of the anti-royal Rupert Murdock became increasingly obsessive in pursuing such "tabloid gold."

The London tabloids were routinely lambasted as the "gutter press" and the Royal Rat Pack. But they ultimately received surprisingly high marks for having exposed some sordid details about Charles and Diana. Indeed, one conservative editor remarked that their tenacious reporters had achieved a greater success rate than political reporters (*The Wall Street Journal* January 29, 1996, p. A-4).

Royal Enigmas

An enigmatic question constantly confronted Elizabeth II: "What does being 'royal' mean at a period in Western history when royalty no longer rules?" The resulting boredom and misgivings invited behavioral and psychological problems for the Queen's family. The Queen's embarrassment increased when her two younger sons, Prince Andrew and Prince Edward, seemed to be veering out of control -- coupled with the splashy nightlife of Sarah, Andrew's wife (Chapter 27).

A respected national poll reported in January 1997 that 48 percent of Brits believed the royal family would be abolished in 50 years. Furthermore, at least a third of those questioned felt that Charles would make a bad king.

Royal Adultery

The media took on the issue of royal adultery during the "War of the Waleses." It had been kept quiet by prior monarchs. Queen Victoria, the architect of strict Victorian morals, reluctantly accepted it. In this age, however, the Queen could not resort to the draconian solution of Henry VIII for solving marital woes, notwithstanding prior decrees.

- The 1351 Statute of Treasons (still on the books) states that any person who violates the wife of the heir to the throne is guilty of high treason.
- The Royal Marriages Act, passed by George III, made it unlawful for his misbehaved children to get married without his consent. One was the future George IV and his wife (previously Caroline of Brunswick, a German Princess), both of whom were notorious adulterers.

Public Relations

Queen Elizabeth managed to exercise exceptional control over information about the royal family, having secured pledges from all members of the staff not to divulge information about their service. Although she held copyright to any letters written by them while employed by the royal family, there were some notable defectors (see below).

Even so, a Market and Opinion Research International poll taken in November 1995 suggested that public respect for the royal family had slipped more sharply than for any profession in the 1990s -- including teachers and social workers. Similar sentiments echoed from this side of the Atlantic. One reader wrote *Newsweek* (April 1, 1996, p. 12) about "these pathetic, anachronistic, meaningless and self-serving stars in their own wretched soap opera."

The Queen took a bold step in March 1997 by going online with a Buckingham Palace royal home page on the Internet. The web site is http://www.royal.gov.uk. Its 150 pages contain official biographies (excluding Sarah, Duchess of York), photos (including the Crown Jewels and Buckingham Palace), various historical facts, and even the royal art collection. But surfers must anticipate that while the Windsors might be accessible in this manner, they are not likely to interact via e-mail.

Airing the Royal Couple's Dirty Laundry

Wendy Berry, former housekeeper of the Royal Couple, broke a confidentiality agreement by writing her book, *The Housekeeper's Diary* (Barricade), which was banned in Britain. She had worked for them from 1985 to 1993. Berry then left England and remained in hiding. Here are a few intimate facts for the curious:

- The royal linen was changed every five days.
- Diana occasionally washed a dish... but not the Prince.
- The Royals got fresh towels every time they washed their hands.
- The valet of the Prince and the dresser of the Princess were solely responsible for touching and handwashing the royal boxer shorts and panties.

A Palm Beach Riddle: Do They...

Or Don't They?

A series of contradictory headlines appeared over several weeks in our local newspapers. The *Palm Beach Daily News* (December 26, 1994, p. 1) carried this headline: "Charles, Diana Join Mar-a-Lago Club, Trump Says." The feature indicated that the Prince and Princess of Wales had joined this prestigious club on Palm Beach being formed by Donald Trump. "The rich and the famous" who presumably had become members included former President Gerald Ford, Henry Kissinger, Steven Spielberg, Sylvester Stallone, Arnold Schwarzenegger, Elizabeth Taylor, Denzel Washington, Lee Iacocca and Norman Mailer.

According to the information provided by Kathy Merlin, Trump's membership director, Charles and Diana had decided to take advantage of a pre-opening membership for "only" $50,000. Moreover, each allegedly signed up individually despite the fact that married couples could receive a two-for-one membership price. The director indicated that this represented a bargain inasmuch as the cost for joining would go up to $75,000 on January 1, 1995.

Buckingham Palace vehemently denied that the Prince and Princess had joined. *The Palm Beach Post* later carried this headline: "Trump's Princely Claim a King-Size Fib, Palace Says" (December 29, 1994, p. B-1). A spokesman at Buckingham Palace stated: "This story is nonsense -- absolutely, utterly untrue. Neither of them is a member" (*Palm Beach Daily News* December 30, 1994, p. 1). He identified himself as the Duty Press Secretary for Her Majesty The Queen. But membership director Merlin maintained that she was telling the truth.

This matter offered more manna for the sensationalist media. *The Palm Beach Post* asserted: "It's blue blood vs. new blood" (December 29, 1994, p. A-16). It then proposed one answer to the question raised by bluebloods on Palm Beach as to why British royalty would hobnob with The Donald: "They have much in common... real estate. For example, *they've* got a tower; *he's* got a tower."

I received further insight about this situation before giving a lecture to the Palm Beach Rotary Club on December 29, 1994. The club president asked for a show of hands by members regarding whom they believed. Trump got one vote. All the others sided with Buckingham Palace.

"The Shiny Sheet" printed another headline one week later: "Trump Backs Down on Chuck and Di 'Memberships'" (*Palm Beach Daily News* January 7, 1995, p. 1). It seems that Trump offered them "honorary" memberships, but no reply had yet been received.

Marital Rift of the Royal Couple

Local Anglophiles became annoyed over the details in the marital rift involving the Royal Couple. This "battle royal" between Charles and Diana appeared in "his books" and "her books"... authorized or not.

Diana appeared to suffer the most, especially in view of having experienced the tragedy of divorce in her own family.

- She suffered severe depression after the birth of her first child, Prince William -- with little support from "the establishment I married into."
- Bulimia became her "release valve" for three years. (This model-thin woman considered herself fat.) One writer indicated that she used Prozac® to control bulimia... resulting in subsequent reference to "the Prozac Princess."
- Diana allegedly had tried to commit suicide because of a loveless marriage (Chapter 31).
- There were regular consultations with astrologers and clairvoyants.

A Field Day for Journalists

The ongoing marital difficulties of the Royal Couple held a fascination for many tabloid readers. It was clear that the fault was not unilateral. Prince Charles had a mistress for many years (see below). Diana, 12 years his junior, indulged her fondness for rock concerts, stage shows and a Mayfair nightspot called Annabel's. She later acknowledged, "We both made mistakes."

A succession of books bashed Prince Charles, Princess Diana, or both.

- Lady Colin Campbell wrote two volumes, *Diana in Private* and *The Royal Marriages* (published by St. Martin's Press), focusing on difficulties in maintaining successful marriages by members of the royal family. It was inevitable that Campbell would visit Palm Beach to sign her books (*Palm Beach Daily News* December 7, 1993, p. 1).
- *The Prince of Wales* by Jonathan Dimbleby provided other revelations. This "authorized" biography claimed that the Prince of Wales never loved Diana, but had married her as a result of pressure from a cold and distant father.

Separation

In an extended documentary broadcast to his nation, the Prince of Wales finally admitted that he had committed adultery once the relationship "became irretrievably broken down" (*The New York Times* June 30, 1994, p. A-6). This occasion also marked the 25th anniversary of his investiture as the Prince of Wales.

The separation of Charles and Diana widened when Camilla Parker Bowles announced her forthcoming divorce from Brigadier Andrew Parker Bowles in January 1995. Charles and Camilla had carried on a steamy relationship for more than two decades. Diana sensed that "There were three of us in this marriage, so it was a bit crowded" (*The Palm Beach Post* November 21, 1995, p. A-10).

Experts on British law could find no constitutional impediment to prevent Charles from ascending to the throne if he were to divorce Diana and then marry Camilla. One political scientist indicated that Charles, as Monarch, could marry anyone other than a Roman Catholic.

> The Prince faced a dilemma when his mother <u>and</u> the Queen Mother refused his request to bring Camilla Parker Bowles to official functions held at their residences. Although the Queen Mother did not object to Bowles as a person, she sought to prevent her grandson from divorcing Princess Diana while he remained heir to the throne (*The Miami Herald* September 18, 1995, p. A-2).

In the ensuing game of "royal roulette," Charles partied in public with his mistress, while a more sexy Diana --

with short skirts and daring necklines -- returned to the spotlight to counter her homewrecker image (*People* November 6, 1995). Her friendship with Will Carling, a rugby star, compounded this perception when he split from his wife. Diana then confessed to a tryst with Army Major James Hewitt, her former riding instructor, in a startling BBC interview aired on November 20, 1995.

Several racy hoaxes complicated matters. <u>Two</u> Diana look-alikes appeared on British and American tabloid TV cavorting in various ways with Hewitt look-alikes. Both "Dianas" apologized to the Princess over the veddy embarrassment so created.

Fortunately, a sprinkling of humor lessened the impact of this rift on Anglophiles.

- One episode was captioned "Diana Taken For Granite" (*The Palm Beach Post* February 15, 1989, p. A-1). The Prince had received a gift from sculptor Sam Tonkiss, depicting a bust, on his visit to northern England. When Charles asked, "Who is it?", Tonkiss replied, "It's your wife, Sir."
- Diana faced other embarrassing media encounters. For instance, a press release by the Canadian Museum of Nature identified her as the "Princess of Whales."
- Diana decided to swear off men because every involvement with a member of the opposite gender ended in "sm, tears and innuendo" according to *The Mirror*. She now became "the Princess of Chastity."

Divorce

An angry Queen Elizabeth II finally had enough of the spectacle of soiled royal linen being washed in public. On December 20, 1995, she ordered Prince Charles and Diana to sever their 14-year marriage through divorce, and end this "malice in the palace." There had been a precedent in the 18th Century when George I divorced his wife before assuming the throne.

Diana offered two dramatic comments during her BBC public confession: (a) "My wish is that my husband finds peace of mind, and from that follows other things"; and (b) she didn't believe she ever would be queen except "in people's hearts."

An aftermath of this interview was the transformation of a fairy-tale princess image into a contemporary role model for feminists who received little sympathy and understanding from their husbands or in-laws (Chapter 30).

Speaking of models, Diana began to consider auctioning her "discarded" evening gowns to raise money for favorite charities... a project that could fetch millions. This came to pass in June 1997 when Christie's auctioned these "rejects" for large sums, especially to persons wishing to own "a bit of Diana" (Chapter 19 and 29). One would-be buyer was a blond, black and statuesque transvestite.

The royal family and the British fashion industry had mixed reactions to any radical shift in clothes preferences by Diana. This possibility loomed large when the new Labor government under Prime Minister Tony Blair seemed intent upon abandoning dress conventions that had signified dignity, elegance and pageantry.

- Harold Brooks-Baker, publisher of *Burke's Peerage*, was horrified at the thought of the Queen wearing a negligee to the state opening of Parliament (*The Wall Street Journal* May 27, 1997, p. B-1).
- Harrods, London's posh apartment store, had to consider the possibility that Diana's sartorial emphasis might violate its strict dress code -- especially the exposure of excess flesh.

Some analysts felt that Diana had missed the basic point: termination of her essential services after having transmitted the Windsor genes to two sons. It was punned that she had supplied "an heir and a spare."

The theme of "the silent princess," whose main function is to produce a male heir to ensure "the succession," exists in other contemporary cultures. An example is Princess Masako of Japan, wife of Crown Prince Naruhito. Her talents as a *magna cum laude* graduate of Harvard, and an evolving respected diplomate speaking five languages fluently, were clearly subordinated to the fertility issue as the populace expressed increasing anxiety when Masako (now 32) had not conceived three years after the wedding.

Charles and Diana untied the royal knot on August 28, 1996, two years after their separation. The divorce in a basement office cost $31, and took five minutes... a far cry from the lavish 1981 wedding spectacle. A legal clerk at the Family Division of the High Court issued the decree that the divorce was now "absolute." At the time, Diana was in Kensington Palace, and Charles 500 miles away at the royal family's Balmoral estate in Scotland.

The press embellished details about the ending of this royal fairy-tale as Diana joined "the first wives club" (popularized by the hit movie), and Charles personified Britain's first husbands club.

- Charles would need permission of Queen Elizabeth and Parliament in the event he sought to remarry before becoming king.
- The Di-vested woman would receive about $25 million from Charles and the Queen, and keep her flat in Kensington Palace and the right to use aircraft from the royal squadron.
- Diana would lose the title, "Her Royal Highness"... now being designated Diana, the Princess of Wales. Accordingly, she would be obliged to curtsy to members of the royal family -- including her ex-husband and two children!
- Diana then was left without a formal prayer. The Queen issued a decree on November 21, 1996 that removed her name from the Church of England's prayer for the royal family.

The "fairy tale" allusion offered journalists and cartoonists more manna. A repeated theme averred that they might live happily ever after... but not with each other. Fleet Street later romantically linked Diana with Hasnat Khan, a Pakistani heart doctor (*The Miami Herald* May 29, 1997, p. A-2).

Diana perhaps reflected on being shortchanged in comparison to American-style divorce, which embodies the concept of shared wealth. By contrast, British law protected Charles' assets with a so-called millionaire's law that enables wealthy spouses to make relatively cheap divorce settlements.

- Amy Irving, the actress, received about $100 million for her 3-year marriage to Steven Spielberg.
- The wife of actor Kevin Costner sought $40 million after 16 years of marriage.
- Patricia Kluge, wife of the richest American (with a net worth of $5.2 billion), received $1 billion plus a 45-room Georgian mansion on 9.9 acres.

Unflattering references to changes in the personality of Princess Diana ought to be evaluated in the context of ongoing severe stress. Jenni Rivett, Diana's friend and trainer, told the *Sunday Mirror* that "her temper and mood swings are incredible" (*The Miami Herald* April 8, 1997, p. A-2).

Although there were no constitutional hurdles to the remarriage of Charles, he and Camilla were preparing the ground for a non-royal "morganatic" marriage. This would enable them to live a "more honest and contented life together" (*The Palm Beach Post* June 30, 1997, p. A-2). The legislation required to amend a 1772 act of Parliament would presumably overcome popular hostility to their wedding.

Operetta Echos

Henry Anatole Grunwald, former editor-in-chief of Time Inc., perceptively captured a recurring theme in his *Wall Street Journal* article titled, "Charles and Diana: Not an Operetta" (July 23, 1996, p. A-20). He focussed on the delightful works of Sigmund Romberg, Rudolph Friml, Franz Lehar and others who had enthralled the world with "romantic confections" involving star-crossed lovers whose painful sense of duty caused them to part.

The classic example is Prince Karl Franz, heir to the German throne, in Romberg's *The Student Prince*. After falling in love with Kathy, an innkeeper's daughter, while attending Heidelberg University, Karl receives word that his father has died. He anguishes between the prospect of marrying a suitably noble bride and his declaration of responsibility: "The path of duty is straight before me. I am the King!" Kathy reinforces this tradition by exclaiming, "Your life belongs to your people."

A similar sentiment reverberates through other operettas (*Her Highness Goes Waltzing*), plays (*The Swan*), and movies (*Roman Holiday*). The underlying issue implies that there is no guarantee of happiness in any royal marital contract when political and social obligations are foremost. The abdication of Edward VIII for Wallis Simpson (Chapter 2) provides one ultimate real-life resolution of such conflict.

More Problems for the Queen

Elizabeth II faced numerous other personal problems that could contribute to fatigue. Their onset could reasonably have been dated 1992, her "annus horribilis" -- referring to the marital collapses of Philip and Andrew, and wide criticism of the royal family's free-spending life styles.

Part of the Queen's despair also involved loss of her figure, causing Her Majesty to be placed on a low-cholesterol diet. An unidentified source at Buckingham Palace stated: "She is certainly missing some of her favorite foods" (*The Palm Beach Post* July 17, 1995, p. A-2).

A "royal scam" involved Raymond Brassard, a Montreal radio host. He managed to interview Queen Elizabeth for 17 minutes on a variety of subjects ranging from the Quebec referendum to her Halloween plans (*The Palm Beach Post* October 28, 1995). Her Majesty had been duped into believing she was taking a private call from Prime Minister Jean Chretien.

More On Fergie

The Queen had to contend with another major marital conflict involving her children -- the separation and divorce of Prince Andrew and Sarah Ferguson. She undoubtedly anguished over the alleged dalliance of Sarah with a Texas millionaire while pregnant with Eugenie. An editorialist for *The Sunday Times* of London described her "puerile nature and incontinent ways" and "louche and loose" behavior.

Terms such as "The Duchess of Pork" and "Freeloader Fergie" indicated her fall from grace as the once-deified became vilified. In a partly self-deprecating biography, *My Story*, Sarah described herself as a "national disgrace" who was not fit for royal life (*The Miami Herald* November 12, 1996, p. A-2).

Sarah was forced to reduce her freebie work in order "to provide my daughters with a pleasant upbringing" (*The Miami Herald* June 1, 1995, p. A-2). The most famous redhead since Lucille Ball confided that this financial strain required visiting a psychiatrist weekly to "help me keep my serenity and face up to my problems." Her debts allegedly exceeded $5.5 million.

The royal family's concern intensified when the now-divorced Duchess of York became more distraught over other mounting personal problems. She was anticipating publication of a book that allegedly revealed intimate details of her affair with John Bryan, a former "financial adviser" (*The Palm Beach Post* October 6, 1996, p. A-14). In the meantime, an infamous picture of Bryan sucking the toe of the topless Duchess had been printed in newspapers and magazines worldwide. Queen Elizabeth ordered a round-the-clock suicide watch after Fergie spent hours "weeping hysterically" behind her locked bedroom door.

The tenacious and resourceful Fergie then attempted to overcome her financial problems in the United States because many on this side of the Atlantic remain enamored with the combination of nobility and celebrity. This contrasted with the pariah's vulgarity status in England where any endorsement was likely to make persons cringe.

> Allan Starkie, author of *Fergie: Her Secret Life*, did have some confidence in her sales appeal for Brits, but with reservations. He added, "She'll end up becoming the lowest common denominator spokesperson for cheaper and cheaper goods" (*The Palm Beach Post* November 25, 1996).

Here are some of Sarah's enterprises.

- One solution involved promoting Weight Watchers for a reported $1 million (*The Wall Street Journal* January 16, 1997, p. B-11).
- Fergie also hawked for hard cash by promoting Ocean Spray cranberry juice and endorsing Olympus cameras.
- She wrote a syndicated column for The New York Times Syndicate (see below) "about subjects close to my heart" -- with emphasis on children's issues and her travels. (The column would avoid the royal family.)

The royal family touched base again with Palm Beach when the foregoing column written by this ostracized member appeared in the *Palm Beach Daily News*. The Duchess of York provided these insights and comments in its May 25, 1997 issue (p. A-6).

- She reaffirmed the motto woven into her wedding dress, "Ex Adversitas Felicitas Crecit" ("Out of Adversity comes Happiness").
- She reminisced that in attempting to please others when public life swallowed her up "like Jonah," she lost touch with her own needs.
- Responding to criticism for giving commercial endorsements, Fergie offered no excuses or defenses. She regarded the denigration of "commercialism" as a luxury suitable only for persons born into wealth.
- The Duchess made it clear that she had intentionally excluded Great Britain in her commercial activities for two reasons. First, she wished to avoid offending the House of Windsor. Second, she was a British parent.

The Duchess' column of August 17, 1997 (*Palm Beach Daily News*, p. A-2) interested many Palm Beachers. Fergie confessed a cardinal error one decade previously: believing her own press -- especially the analogy of being "a breath of fresh air" for Buckingham Palace. After being stripped down "into a flat cartoon character" and losing her "HRH," the Duchess began to discover her real self. She took particular pride in the fact that the children still loved her "with or without a tiara."

Princess Diana and the Duchess of York became ex-soul sisters, as well as ex-sisters-in-law, after the publication of *My Story*. Diana accused her of "betraying my trust and friendship... to sell your book" (*The Miami Herald* July 6, 1997, p. A-2). They had not spoken since it was published in November 1996.

Ms. Ferguson may be ultimately best remembered for her statement: "When you have touched the flames of hell, a branding iron is only a mild inconvenience."

A Palm Beach Solution

Anglophiles in Palm Beach weighed the options available to the royal family. Helen Bernstein-Fealy, a feature writer for the *Palm Beach Daily News*, offered a solution: all members should move to Palm Beach (November 26, 1995, p. A-10). She explained:

> "We have some here now, so they wouldn't be lonely. We have polo, and Prince Charles comes frequently to play in Wellington or Vero Beach.
>
> "The Breakers is almost as large as Buckingham Palace and they could buy it and change it to become more suitable. We have drawbridges that could be opened to exclude undesirables. The real estate market could benefit by having them here...
>
> "Queen Elizabeth could finally retire from all her ceremonial duties and play croquet court. Prince Philip could do whatever he does over there. They could join Mar-a-Lago, which would make Donald Trump happy."[1]

Local writers offered many tongue-in-cheek opportunities for Diana in view of her stated wish to remain "queen of people hearts." Loretta Grantham listed eleven -- including goodwill ambassador for <u>Royal</u> Palm Beach, imperial employment for <u>Royal</u> Caribbean cruise ships, and proofreader of fairy tales at <u>Crown</u> Books (*The Palm Beach Post* March 23, 1996, p. D-1).

[1]©1995 *Palm Beach Daily News*. Reproduced with permission.

29

Di-vestment by a Fashion Icon

Only a moment; a moment of strength, of romance, of glamour -- of youth!
Joseph Conrad
(*Youth*) (1902)

Princess Diana became a legitimate world-class fashion icon. Her gowns, hair styles and related embellishments, especially those worn during visits to Palm Beach and Washington (Chapter 19), impacted on the attire of many fashionable women here and abroad.

Evolution of the Queen of Style

Diana matured emotionally and gained self-confidence after her bitter encounters with the royal family. She evidenced a concomitant transition from wearing conventional extremes. The Princess challenged the world of fashion through increasingly daring styles, with emphasis on understated grandeur -- including a knack for making simple evening sheaths appear highly attractive. Diana preferred revealing and elegant form-fitting garments. As with many women, she had to experiment in order to determine which styles felt most comfortable and looked good on her... generally with emphasis on minimalism.

Clothes As a Vent for Emotion
Clothes also empowered the Princess to exert subtle revenge as an antidote to severe emotional pain.

> Diana arrived in a sexy dress for a gala dinner at London's Serpentine Gallery on June 29, 1994. It was the night Charles admitted his longstanding affair with Camilla Parker Bowles (Chapter 28). Di supporters termed this black thigh-baring Christina Stambolian gown with cup sleeves "the up-yours dress." Her stunning appearance belied the fact that she had bought it off the rack for a 1993 dinner.

Di-vestment

After parting from her two-timing husband and hostile in-laws (Chapter 28 and 30), Diana saw no need to remain a royal clotheshorse. The less-than-merry princess then decided to unload the raft of garments collected over 15 years.

> Diana apparently came to terms with a truism I have uttered many times to wealthy Palm Beach patients: "The more you own, the more it owns you." This advice and the ensuing behavioral modification by patients appear in my recent book, HEALTH AND WEALTH, PALM BEACH STYLE (Sunshine Sentinel Press).

Another consideration kept recurring to me. Was the Princess being turned off from "the tyranny of fashion" -- illustrated by "Park Avenue Dominatrix"? It featured giant shoulder pads, skin-tight leather pants, and minis with hip-high slits, fishnet stockings, and high stilettos. I suspected that the thought of dressing as an animal repelled Diana.

Diana offered 79 of her famous frocks for auction by Christie's in New York to benefit several favorite charities. (This idea had been the brainchild of Prince William, her oldest son.) The decision coincided with Diana's ongoing deemphasis of a lifestyle requiring formal gowns, and immersion in charity work as herself -- uncoiffed, unbejewelled, and with a minimum of makeup.

News of the June 25, 1997 auction of "Dresses from the Collection of Diana, Princess of Wales" traveled fast and wide. The firm had sold nearly $1.6 million worth of its glossy 204-page catalogs one week before the event. They were priced at $250 for the limited hardbound edition, and $60 for the soft-cover one -- the cost of admission to view the exhibition. The proceeds were earmarked for cancer and AIDS activities.

Most of these dresses had been made by Britain's outstanding designers. They included Victor Edelstein, Zandra Rhodes and especially Catherine Walker.

Diana attended a $250 invitation-only fund-raiser two nights before the auction. It combined a champagne reception and private viewing of the collection. No press photographers or *paparazzi* (Chapter 30) were allowed. The first person Diana greeted was Palm Beach-based handbag designer Lana Marks (Chapter 32), whose friendship began with the making of a special luxury handbag.

As in the case of Jackie Onassis' belongings, these items became HOT -- regardless of size and fit -- because of the many photos of Diana wearing them. Interested buyers regarded her fairy-tale gowns as potential purchases of a lifetime. Ellen Louise Petho, who spent more than $100,000 for four dresses, told *The New York Post*: "I'll never wear them. They shouldn't be worn. These are for history."

- The aforementioned gown nicknamed by Brits as "the up-yours dress" sold for $74,000.
- Linda Ann Boyle, a West Palm Beach real estate agent, had a different thought. If her bid was successful, she said, "I'd wear it to bed" (*The Palm Beach Post* June 26, 1997, p. A-9).

This royal rummage sale proved successful... raising $3.25 million. In effect, Diana had become the "Princess of Sales" despite her absence at the actual auction.

> With reference to the "as is" nature of the gowns, one buyer paid $66,300 for a Catherine Walker blue-and-white satin cocktail dress that was pilled and frayed from considerable wear.

About 83 percent of the successful bids for gowns worn by the "Queen of Style" came from Americans, especially Southerners and Midwesterners. For me, this affirmed the appropriateness of the book's subtitle, AMERICA'S FASCINATION WITH "THE TOUCH OF ROYALTY."

The "losers," however, were not in total despair. Some with proportions larger than those of Diana indicated they might be in the market if Fergie decided to auction off her dresses.

The Winning Bidder

Maureen Rorech, a 37-year-old Tampa businesswomen, dodged the press for three months after it learned that "an unidentified Florida woman" bought 13 of the 79 gowns during that "Wednesday night fever." She spent nearly one million dollars -- including $222,500 for the midnight-blue-velvet Victor Edelstein gown the Princess had worn to the White House state dinner, and in which she danced with another icon, John Travolta (Chapter 20). (Some speculated that this star of *Saturday Night Fever* bought it.) The other dresses cost her $40,000-$50,000 each.

Rorech owned four upscale women's clothing boutiques (called M), and a high-end furniture/accessory store (Moda For the Home). She had made her successful bids to Christie's by phone... thereby shattering most home-shopping records.

This single mother took her three sons (the oldest being nine) to a Long Island airport hangar where she picked up the gowns. They were stored in a Tampa bank vault. Contrary to most of the other successful bidders, Diana's size 8 gowns were too large for the tiny Rorech.

Rorech preferred the designation "guardian" of the gowns, rather than "owner." The phenomenal interest in these new possessions became evident when her Web site (www.princessdigowns.com) averaged 70,000 hits in the days after the tragedy.

Rorech also lent Diana's gowns for a 24-month exhibit that would go from Florida (including Palm Beach County) to London. This "International Queen of Hearts Dress Tour" was set up by the nonprofit People's Princess Charitable Foundation to benefit AIDS and cancer research.

The Historical Society of Palm Beach County already was the repository of 83 gowns by Arnold Scaasi, the famous fashion designer. This part-time Palm Beacher offered them for its permanent collection in March 1997. The designs had been worn by First Lady Barbara Bush and local clients -- including Marylou Whitney, Eles Gilet, Betty Scripps and the late Mary Sanford (*Palm Beach Daily News* September 30, 1997, p. 1).

A Good Investment

The amounts paid for Diana's gowns seemed outrageous to many at the time. But they proved great bargains following her death. Sotheby's estimated that <u>each</u> of these dresses now might fetch $2 million to $5 million!

To place such "Diana dementia" in perspective, a rich Kuwaiti offered $1 million for the mangled vehicle recovered in the Paris "tunnel of doom."

Homage Via Postage Stamps

Entrepreneurs quickly recognized the inherent commercial value of photos featuring Diana wearing these now-famous gowns. International Collectors Society of Owings Mills (Maryland) became the exclusive worldwide distributor of a set of nine Limited Edition postage stamps showing her in such attire. These colorful stamps, four times larger than a regular U.S. stamp, were legal for postage in the Togolaise Republic. Issued just days before her death (Chapter 30), their value increased dramatically. Similar stamps and first-day covers by other firms followed in short order (Chapter 30).

Section VII

THE DEATH OF PRINCESS DIANA

The rich, the poor, the great, the small are Levell'd.
Death confounds 'em all.

John Gay (1685-1732)
(*Fables*)

To an amazing degree, society is saved by the unusual person.

James Michener
(*The Miami Herald*, September 27, 1987, p. C-3)

30

The "People's Princess"
A Tragic Closure

...how are the might fallen!
Samuel II (1:19)

She was beautiful, she was good, and she was flawed.
Comment of Aaron Frankel
(*The Miami Herald*
September 20, 1997, p. G-5)

I occasionally conjectured about the nature of the reception that Diana, whether single or remarried, would receive on returning to Palm Beach. With expansion of her role as "The People's Princess" for deserving causes in Britain and elsewhere, I doubted that the local scene would hold enough priority without the inducement of some fund-raiser benefitting her favored charities and projects. They included AIDS, cancer, heart disease, the continued threat of land mines that killed or maimed 26,000 persons annually, and the plight of battered women, suffering children and the homeless.

I subsequently learned of TWO events that Princess Diana was scheduled to attend during the following February and March.

- Lana Marks (Chapter 32) had been planning a gala fund-raiser honoring Diana at The Breakers on February 18, 1998. This private and non-affiliated event was projected to raise up to three million dollars in support of her causes. Every prominent Palm Beacher who had been asked to join the organizing committee "jumped at the idea" (*The Palm Beach Post* September 12, 1997, p.E-1).
- Helen Boehm, a Palm Beacher who had presented Diana with a porcelain replica (made by her company) of the bouquet she carried at her wedding, bemoaned Diana's absence aboard the QE2 for the forthcoming Red Cross fund-raiser. She stated, "It won't be the same" (*Palm Beach Daily News* September 4, 1997, p. 3).

Few could deny the assertion that Diana was indeed "the most photographed woman in the world." *People* Magazine had featured her photo on its cover 43 times! Elizabeth Taylor was a distant second (14 covers). *Time* and *Newsweek* each put her on their front covers seven times -- thereby placing Diana in the category of Jacqueline Onassis and Grace Kelly.

Diana trusted her instincts and personal sense of *noblesse oblige* as an international ambassador of goodwill when championing causes close to her heart. She held the hands of lepers and AIDS victims, and consoled the terminally ill in ways that seemed utterly sincere. Diana's pursuit of good deeds in her "new life" reminded me of these lines in *The Lady's Not For Burning* (Oxford University Press) by Christopher Fry:

All my friends tell me I actually exist.
And by an act of faith I have come to believe them.

Fate Intervenes

These violent delights have violent ends.
Shakespeare
(*Romeo and Juliet*)

But fate intervened on August 30, 1997. Diana was killed in a high-speed crash in a Paris tunnel along the Seine as it passes under the Place de l'Alma to the Place de la Concorde. She and her fatally injured companion, Dodi Fayed, were being pursued by *paparazzi* (see below) on motorcycles.

<u>The New Friend</u>

Subsequent revelations about the alleged courtship of Diana and the 42-year-old Fayed enhanced the tragedy.

The Princess had recently given him two highly sentimental gifts -- her late father's cufflinks, and a gold cigar clipper with a tag inscribed, "With love from Diana."

Dodi wrote a poem for Diana. It was then inscribed on a silver plaque that Dodi placed under a pillow in his Paris apartment. Dodi's parents later presented it to the Spencer family with the request that it be placed in her coffin... its words never made public.

Fayed also presented Diana with a magnificent diamond "friendship ring" (valued at $205,400) over dinner at the Ritz Hotel in Paris that Saturday evening. It was recovered from the crashed car.

- The ring had been made by the Paris jeweler Albert Repossi.
- The couple briefly visited the Monaco branch of his store ten days prior to the accident -- already knowing the object of Diana's desire from an advertisement in a high-fashion magazine.
- Fayed picked up the ring, which had been altered to Diana's size, at the firm's Paris store on August 30... six hours before the crash.
- Repossi stated that Dodi indicated he wanted to spend the rest of his life with Diana. Through this curious twist of fate, he did... albeit for a brief period.
- The existence of the ring surfaced because Repossi's insurance policy with Lloyd's required him to file a claim within 24 hours for an unexpected loss because he had not yet been paid.

The Paparazzi

*A picture may be worth a thousand words, but a
thousand pictures are not worth even one life.*
Palm Beach Jewish Times
September 5, 1997, p.11

This eponym for photographic bounty hunters means "waste paper." It apparently originated with Signore Paparazzo, a side walk photographer in Federico Fellini's *La Dolce Vita* ("The Sweet Life"). The 1960 film about decadence focused on a gossip columnist played by Marcello Mastroianni.

These free-lance commercial photographers cater to a worldwide tabloid culture of voyeurism. They focus on persons living in "the fast lane," for whose stolen glimpses readers thirst. About 50 of this ilk constantly stalked Diana in Britain despite repeated pleas not to invade her private life. Their arrogant behavior at home even caused Diana to consider moving away from England before they "hounded her to death."

This genre of photographers persisted in being obnoxious intruders because of the lure of wealth -- even from one lucky shot. For example, a picture showing Diana embracing Dodi at St. Tropez in August 1997 fetched more than $3.2 million (!) worldwide (*The Miami Herald* September 12, 1997, p.E-8).

Speaking from her own experience, Princess Grace of Monaco jokingly warned Diana that such publicity hounding would "get a lot worse."

Reflections on a Faustian Bargain

Heated confrontations with *paparazzi* by persons who sought -- and then achieved -- great fame provide a contemporary morality lesson that could be equated with a Faustian bargain.

Diana's experiences were replays of encounters by personalities such as Elvis Presley, Sylvester Stallone, Marilyn Monroe, Brigitte Bardot, Marlon Brando and John Lennon. All had been taunted and "looned" by obnoxious photographers bent on having them lose their "cool."

Photographers "doing Di" waited in trees, bushes, phone booths, nearby apartments, and even on ladders propped over walls. In view of the high price on her photographed head, some boarded the next plane or train on learning of her departure from paid spies.

Diana and the other celebrities seriously pondered this matter. Was extreme hounding by media fanatics too great a price to pay for a phenomenon variously called "the frenzy of renown" (Leo Braudy) and "the fine print of fame" (Clark Gable)?

Worldwide Grief

In virtual disbelief, a shocked world manifested deep grief. This tragedy assumed Shakespearean proportions. Unlike Macbeth and Hamlet, however, it might have been averted (Chapter 31).

Millions mourned the out-of-the-blue death of this 36-year-old princess who embodied great beauty and benevolence, notwithstanding her humiliation by members of the royal family. Long queues waited up to ten hours to sign condolence books.

Most Britons felt that their country -- and the world -- had been cheated of the potential they expected from a mature and vibrant Diana with the Everywoman touch. They singled out withdrawal of the title "Her Royal Highness" as an arbitrary "shabby" and "petty" insult. This "New Age Princess" had tried to bridge the enormous gap between "them" and "us" after her post-divorce release from a personal, social and political near-execution in a quasi-Tower of London.

> The matter of "royal blood" held a unique sting for Queen Elizabeth II, especially after publication of Kitty Kelley's book, *The Royals*. She resurrected the contention that the sickly King George VI and his wife had Elizabeth and sister Margaret through artificial insemination after failing to conceive in the usual manner.

The impact on adoring fans became even more overwhelming in the context of Diana's dedication to her two sons (ages 15 and 12), her avowed goal of building a productive public career, and the prospect of finally enjoying a romantic life with Fayed. The father of this wealthy movie producer (*Chariots of Fire*) was the owner of London's prestigious Harrods department store.

> Many likened the intensity of the spontaneous public mourning that ensued to the experience of persons on first learning that President John F. Kennedy had been assassinated.

There were several remarkable coincidences, including that of Diana's age.

- The Spencers, Diana's family, were quintessential English aristocrats. Their lineage dated back to 1603 -- the last year of the reign of Elizabeth I. Her mother, Anne Boleyn, had been beheaded at the age of 36 by King Henry VIII (her father). The decapitated body was then buried with other state prisoners in an unmarked grave.
- Marilyn Monroe also died at 36. Elton John, the popular singer, had composed a song in her memory during 1972. He then sang new words, written for Diana by Bernice Taupin, at Westminster Abbey (see below).
- Princess Grace, the wife of Monaco's Prince Rainier, had been killed in a car crash 15 years earlier.

Endearing Young Charms

The biggest disease this world suffers from... (is) people feeling unloved.
Princess Diana, 1985

Britons would require much convincing that their intense and prolonged lamentations largely represented a mass hysteria induced by the media rather than their personal endearment of Diana. A ballet shoe attached to the railing outside Kensington Palace reflected their emotions. Its inscription read, "You were a Cinderella at the Ball, and now you are a Sleeping Beauty."

In a sense, Diana also personified "the American dream" by emerging from relative obscurity, overcoming adversity, and becoming a superstar. "The world's most photographed woman" exhibited the grace and polish of a natural-born socialite, but one who also touched people's hearts. Her romps with sister-in-law Sarah Ferguson, and the desire to dance with John Travolta (star of *Saturday Night Fever*) may have appalled her in-laws, but endeared her to "ordinary" people.

Breaking the royal reticence, Queen Elizabeth belatedly captured some of the foregoing sentiments in her three-minute address the day before the funeral. "I share in your determination to cherish her memory... No one who knew Diana will ever forget her. Millions of others who never met her, but felt they knew her, will remember her." She added that Diana "was an exceptional and gifted human being. In good times and bad, she never lost her capacity to smile and laugh or to inspire others with her warmth and kindness. I admire and respected her for her energy and commitment to others, and especially for her devotion to her two boys."

The Queen's delayed appearance in public after Diana's death seemed consistent with the assertion about her "excellent passive judgment." Furthermore, many British women would have found the Queen more appealing as a person if, like Diana, she had admitted how purportedly difficult her own married life had been while adhering to the noble motto, "I serve."

Terms of Endearment

From the moment my wife and I met Diana on her arrival at Palm Beach International Airport (Chapter 15), we were impressed by her genuine graciousness. Diana's endearment to the people of Britain therefore came as no surprise to us. A few manifestations are recalled.

I.   The Tenacious "Single Mother"

Diana's ability to function successfully as a single mother created a bond with untold numbers of women onto whom the responsibility of raising children had been thrust following rejection, infidelity, depression and divorce. Her societal position and wealth did not undermine such high regard.

Despite prior flaws and indiscretions, Diana became a remarkable transference symbol -- akin to a living Rorschach test -- onto which women could project their fears and their fantasies. They were equally enamored with Diana's attempts to orient William and Harry firsthand to the real world... whether by taking them to visit a hospital or homeless shelter (Chapter 32), or paying for hamburgers bought at McDonalds.

II.   Regaining Self-Esteem

Women could identify with this notable person in other ways. She had worked hard to lose the weight gained during pregnancy, exercised to stay in shape, and rebuilt her confidence -- all the while maintaining friendships (away from the cameras) with "ordinary folk," especially individuals who had suffered great tragedy. This enormous personal achievement will be discussed in Chapter 31.

III.   An Appealing Sense of Humor

Numerous acquaintances mentioned Diana's great sense of targeted humor when asked about their memories of her. The Queen (see above) and Lana Marks, her "personal friend" (Chapter 32), emphasized this attribute.

Many examples of Diana's humor could be cited. One that made an indelible impression was reference to herself as "POW" -- variously interpreted as Princess of Wales and Prisoner of War. Another was her apology to a friend for noise over the phone being caused by an attempt to place a tiara on her head.

Legions of Brits with a green thumb appreciated another funny anecdote. They were enthralled by an affirmative answer from the chief horticulturalist to Diana's spontaneous question during a tour of the Mughal Gardens at the President's palace in New Delhi: "Do you talk to the plants?" Few PR agents could have concocted this spontaneous meaningful query.

IV. Compassion

Diana's compassion for the humble and those with serious afflictions became increasingly manifest. Fans did not denigrate it because of explanations about personal psychological experiences in her own childhood involving a dysfunctional family in which her mother left her father (and four children) for another man (Chapter 31). Moreover, they rejected the notion that such sensitivity was a PR ruse because of awareness that Diana knew the nature of toil for low wages -- namely, one pound (about $1.70) an hour. She had been employed as a cleaner, waitress, chairlady, babysitter, and kindergarten teacher before Charles' proposal.

An illustration of this attitude is illustrated by a 1996 picture taken in Pakistan as she embraced a boy afflicted with advanced cancer. Remembering his face, his voice and his pain, Diana reflected that this particular photo was "very special for me" (*The Palm Beach Post* September 3, 1997, p. D-4). Her action impressed those present because she held the boy on her lap throughout the party given for her, disregarding the stenching odor from his festering tumor.

Pent-up Royal Tensions Over

"The People's Princess"

Some aspects of Diana's life contributed to this unprecedented outpouring of grief. They proved particularly poignant for women who identified with "the princess inside every woman," and a flawed mortal to whom they could relate in terms of occasional self-indulgence with lovely clothes, manipulative activities, emotional outbursts due to neglect, and the love of their children. There was wide respect for her democratic genius in directing herself "downward" as a jeans-clad mother, and for reinventing the concept of royalty involving the "laying on of hands."

Royal Indifference/Neglect and Their Consequences

As a new bride, only 19 years old, Diana received little affection from her husband and the royal family. She later transmitted this emotional void during a BBC interview. Her utterance that the greatest need of humanity was to feel loved -- "even for just a minute or just an hour" -- must have pierced the royal family as devastatingly as an arrow.

Diana was given a paucity of training for the enormous burden she was expected to assume as the Princess of Wales. Some averred that it was less than the basic instructions for a new secretary or checkout clerk.

Even the Queen Mother ("Queen Mum"), who had been instrumental in persuading Charles to marry the demure teenager (after disinterest by Sarah, one of her older sisters), turned against Diana.

> Sarah had met Charles at Ascott during June 1977. It occurred in the wake of her ill-fated romance with the Duke of Westminster. After joining Charles for a skiing party in Switzerland one year later, Sarah stated that she would refuse to marry him if he proposed.

The hostile attitudes of censorious in-laws fostered bitter emotions that became unbearable to a Cinderella whose glass slippers had broke. They culminated clinically in severe depression, eating disorders (anorexia and bulimia), and repeated thoughts of suicide (Chapter 31). One evidence of the inability of her relatives to understand Diana's eating problems was their purported retort that she was wasting food! As a result, Diana sought help from psychoanalysts, new age psychics, astrologers, faith healers and clairvoyants. The special friendship she developed with several close friends, including Lana Marks of Palm Beach (Chapter 32), was probably more beneficial.

A Marital Disaster

The subsequent unraveling of Diana's marriage could be convincingly likened to a self-destruct television mini-series, or a Greek tragedy rescripted for this era. Unfortunately for Diana, "the frog" didn't turn into a handsome prince after the princess kissed him.

British women deeply resented the fact that Diana had to cope with an adulterous husband having "the personality of a herring." This romantic young woman had saved her virginity for the expected love of her life, only to be confronted with evidence that her husband had been having a longstanding clandestine affair with someone else's wife.

Charles' ongoing affair with Camilla Parker-Bowles (alias "the rotweiller") devastated the sensitive first-time-in-love Diana. The facts became convincing. They included meetings during his hunting trips, finding pictures of Camilla in Charles' diary, and the direct line to her on his phone.

Concern Over the New Beau

There was widespread, albeit generally unexpressed, anxiety over Dodi Fayed, Diana's new boyfriend. This Egyptian-born graduate of the Royal Military Academy at Sandhurst traveled with a masseuse and bodyguards.

Mohamed al-Fayed, his father, was alleged to be richer than the Queen. He had lived in London since 1963. In addition to owning Harrods of Knightsbridge, his properties included the Ritz Hotel of Paris, *Punch* magazine, a radio station, the Fulham soccer club, the Balnagow castle in Scotland, and a $24 million yacht.

There was a concerned sense of unease that Diana might be trading her life style for a possibly worse Arab alternative. Her step-grandmother, Dame Barbara Cartland, stated: "My only concern is that this Dodi is a foreigner" (*The New York Times* August 17, 1997, p.5).

Although the British public extended its best wishes to Diana in the belief that she had found love again, it nevertheless had reservations.

- One concerned the reputation of Dodi as an international playboy who didn't pay his bills.
- Many distrusted his alleged wealthy Egyptian ancestry. There was speculation that some of the money used by his father to purchase Harrods had come from the Sultan of Brunei, an associate. Furthermore, the debts of this company increased dramatically by the year ending January 1996.

Diana's Funeral

A crowd flowed over London Bridge, so many, I had not thought death had undone so many.
T. S. Eliot (1922)

I vow to thee, my country, all
earthly things above,
Entire and whole and perfect, the
service of my love:
The love that asks no question, the
love that stands the test,
That lays upon the altar the
dearest and the best.
Favorite hymn of Princess Diana sung at her funeral

Many Brits expressed amazement over their devastating sense of loss, both individually and collectively. The outpouring of grief from school children enhanced this phenomenon.

- Overt crying by men and women replaced the proverbial "stiff upper British lip."
- More than a million bouquets of flowers enveloped Buckingham Palace and Kensington Palace (where Diana had lived).
- Thousands of persons camped outside the night before the funeral, despite rain and cold, to immerse themselves personally in her funeral happening.
- The sight of numerous candles being held in the dark, coupled with improvised little shrines, became unforgettable. It reflected the profound affection for this aristocrat with the common touch... much as with Winston Churchill and President Franklin Roosevelt.

- Several million people of all ages, races, sexual preferences, and socioeconomic groups lined the four-mile route of the cortege shoulder-to-shoulder -- in some places 20-30 deep. The event was likened to a magnet drawing heterogeneous persons, described as "Diana's rainbow coalition," from the entire kingdom.
- The silence of this huge and almost worshipful throng for one hour and 40 minutes -- interrupted only by the hooves of horses, the tenor bell of Westminster Abbey, and occasional wails from grieving women -- was termed "a solemn stampede."

The visual and emotional impact of the funeral cortege and service eclipsed that for the ceremonies of Winston Churchill and Lord Mountbatten. It was particularly traumatic for persons who had seen Diana's wedding 16 years earlier..

Diana lay in 1,500-pound lead-lined coffin drawn by a horse, accompanied by First Battalion Welsh guards in their scarlet tunics... befitting the late Princess of Wales. The coffin was wrapped in the maroon and gold royal standard, covered with white lilies. A small wreath of white roses from Prince Harry, accompanied by his note bearing the word "Mummy," evoked an avalanche of tears.

Another spectacle ensued after the coffin arrived at St. James Palace. About 500 individuals, representing persons who had been touched by their caring "Queen of Hearts" in many causes, joined the procession to Westminster Abbey.

An ironic vignette occurred when the royal flag slipped off its moorings above Buckingham Palace. Falling to half-staff, it became an unintended tribute to Diana. (The Union Jack had been at half-staff all week throughout the country.)

More Evidence of Epic Grief

The entire country joined the hushed crowd in London to observe a minute of silence after the service ended. The concomitant 20 percent drop of electricity used in Britain validated the population's involvement in paying homage to Diana. The magnitude of interest in Diana's funeral overwhelmed the media.

- An estimated 2.5 billion persons heard or watched every detail.
- Nielsen Media Research reported that 12.57 million U.S. households -- some 50 million viewers -- turned into the coverage on four major television networks between 4 AM and 8 AM (Eastern time) that Saturday of the Labor Day weekend. Furthermore, most of the networks did so without commercial interruption to avoid certain criticism from viewers if they tried to exploit the event.

Althorp

Diana's body was taken to Althorp, her family's lush ancestral estate, with its 16th Century mansion, 72 miles north of London. In stark contrast to the mass of humanity in London, only ten persons viewed the burial in newly consecrated ground on an island therein. This decision would enable her family to visit the grave in privacy. It also obviated an inevitable inundation of the tiny nearby village of Great Brington by tourists.

> Twenty previous generations of Spencers were buried in the private Chapel. They included the great-great-grandfather of George Washington, and the ashes of Diana's father who died in 1992.

The Independent newspaper regarded the decision to bury Diana on this small island as appropriate. It commented that her loneliness and vulnerability in life "made her seem so often like an island surrounded by the hostile waters of royal rejection." The hurt extended posthumously when Buckingham Palace sent out feelers about restoring Diana's H.R.H. The Spencer family promptly rejected the idea.

Resolving the Jewish Community's Dilemma

Jewish funerals are forbidden on Saturday... the Sabbath. In the absence of any precedent, the Chief Rabbi of Britain was besieged by calls requesting guidance about properly honoring the Princess of Wales.

Thousands of synagogues throughout the 53-nation Commonwealth conducted services in Diana's memory, concurrent with those at Westminster Abbey. Chief Rabbi Jonathan Sacks requested them to join in "the national mood of remembrance" with a prayer that began, "Almighty God, we come before you today, sharing in the grief of the British people and the world, at the untimely and sudden death of Diana, Princess of Wales."

Observant Jews respected the altruistic commitment of Princess Diana to charitable causes. In the key *Amidah* service, for example, they emphasize support of the fallen, healing the sick, and freeing persons in bondage. Equal emphasis is placed on assisting widows and orphans, and not putting "stumbling blocks" in the way of the blind.

In effect, these benevolent attributes imparted a sense of "Jewishness" to Diana's later life. (Her close American friend, Lana Marks, was Jewish.) Rabbi Chaim Wender of Delray Beach, who had lived in England more than five years, stated in a sermon: "There was a willingness for her to be candid about her own personal suffering which heightened empathy towards others who are suffering" (*Palm Beach Jewish Times* September 12, 1997, p. 12).

Some Highlights of the
Westminster Abbey Service

To everything there is a season.
Ecclesiastes

The funeral service for Diana at Westminster Abbey, scene of many coronations and burials of English leaders, remains permanently etched in the memory of those who attended or viewed it. No member from the House of Windsor spoke, however.

Elton John's Rendition
Elton John, the rock superstar, was a close friend of Diana. In fact, she had recently comforted him -- by lending an arm, and saying some words of support -- during services held during July in Italy for Gianni Versace, the slain fashion designer.

This popular singer evoked a torrent of tears when he performed an updated version of *Candle In the Wind* at a grand piano. The new lyrics (by Bernie Taupin) for *Goodbye, England's Rose* stunned all -- especially "Your candle's burned out long before your legend ever will," and "Now you belong to heaven and the stars spell out your name." Another memorable line was reference to a country "who'll miss the wings of your compassion more than you'll ever know."

The Eulogy by Earl Spencer
Charles Spencer, younger brother of Diana and the ninth Earl Spencer, delivered a searing eulogy. He lashed out at the royal family, the media (the editors of Britain's tabloid newspapers having been banned from the service), and the *paparazzi* in this stunning oration. His cries of anger and pain -- in the presence of the royal family and distinguished guests -- provided an indictment without parallel concerning the manner in which Diana had been treated.

> Another basis for Earl Spencer's intense emotions emerged several days later. Reports suggested that the Queen and Prince Charles had fought over the funeral arrangements. Elizabeth initially demanded that Diana's body <u>not</u> be placed in any of the royal palaces, and insisted on a private service! The latter so infuriated Diana's family that its members refused at first to communicate with Buckingham Palace. Charles' violent disagreement with his mother apparently necessitated mediation from the office of Prime Minister Tony Blair.

Spencer summed his sister's attributes in these memorable words.

> "Diana was the very essence of compassion, of duty, of style, of beauty. All over the world she was a symbol of selfless humanity, a standard-bearer for the rights of the truly downtrodden, a truly British girl who transcended nationality, someone with a natural nobility who was classless, who proved in the last year that she needed no royal title to continue to generate her particular brand of magic.

"Today is our chance to say 'thank you' for the way you brightened our lives, even though God granted you but half a life. We will all feel cheated that you were taken from us so young, and yet we must learn to be grateful that we came along at all."

In essence, Spencer proclaimed, "We gave you our jewel, which you abused. Now we take her back!" The Earl criticized the news media that had made Diana "the most hunted woman on earth," and "used regularly to drive her to tearful despair." (He noted the irony that Diana was the name of the goddess of hunting.) Commenting on this baffling situation, Spencer stated, "My own and only explanation is that genuine goodness is threatening to those at the opposite end of the moral spectrum."

Earl Spencer also had been the target of Fanie Jason, a relentless photo stalker in Cape Town (*The New York Times* October 5, 1997). Jason resorted to various tactics to obtain pictures of Spencer, his estranged wife and children, and a girlfriend. Spencer's suit to inhibit such photography without his permission prompted the Freedom of Expression Institute to underwrite Jason's defense.

These remarks evoked repeated applause both in and outside the Abbey. Many in Hyde Park gave him a standing ovation. Some made an analogy of this seminal oration -- both in terms of content and public reaction -- to that of Marcus Antonius (Marc Anthony) after the slaying of Julius Caesar at the age of 44.

More Tributes to "England's Rose"

Diana's death and funeral received coverage throughout the world. An estimated 2.5 billion persons saw, heard or read about scenes that were as moving as any during the 160-year-old history of the House of Windsor.

Persons from all walks of life were moved to participate in the emotional outpouring for this "aristocrat with an unabashedly bourgeois heart" (*The New York Times* September 7, 1997) -- whether by witnessing the cortege in person, watching the television coverage for days on end, reciting prayers, or through spoken and written comments. John Grogan wrote in the *Sun-Sentinel* (September 3, 1997, p. B-1).

"She was the perfect Everywoman in the perfect fairy tale. And, as it turns out, the perfect tragic heroine... She was a poster child for the maxim that money cannot buy happiness. Sometimes, not even the Princess of Wales can. She reminded us to watch what we wish for. And that lives of obscurity, simply led, can sometimes be the most fulfilling... Our choices have consequences, Diana's life told us. Our choices in love and life, and even in something as ordinary as which car we climb into."[1]

Respect by the Business Community

Several of England's most prestigious businesses made unprecedented decisions to honor Diana as a "mark of respect."

- Harrods closed that Saturday... for the first time in the history of this institution.
- Sotheby's postponed until February 1998 one of the biggest sales in its history: the auction of property previously belonging to the Duke and Duchess of Windsor, which was to have begun on September 11. This event evoked interest comparable to the 1995 sale of items owned by Jacqueline Kennedy Onassis. The Windsor auction included the desk on which then King Edward VIII signed the Instrument of Abdication "for the woman I love."

Even Weight Watchers joined. It cancelled an ad campaign in which Sarah Ferguson (Chapter 28) stated that losing weight is harder than "outrunning the *paparazzi.*"

Contributions

Tangible proof -- in cash -- validated the high affection for Diana. A report on September 9, 1997 stated that the Princess Diana Memorial Trust Fund already had received $240 million! Credit card donations averaged 350 calls an hour.

Renamed Places

Someone will ultimately research the many streets, hospitals, buildings, communities and other places in England and abroad that bear Diana's name to memorialize her. A few are cited.

- The Caribbean island of Montserrat was planning to rebuild after suffering severe damage from volcanic eruptions. It would rename its new capital Port Diana as a lasting tribute to the princess.
- A major street in the beachfront district of Rio De Janeiro was named Princess Diana of Wales Street. This road, leading to one of Rio's spectacular beaches, cut across the residential neighborhood of Sao Cohrado... home to many artists, celebrities and politicians.

Entrepreneurial Heaven

The lucrative appeal of this tragedy involving "the most photographed woman in the world" set off an immediate chain reaction among entrepreneurs, notwithstanding their awareness that such efforts would offend many persons.

- Mention was made in Chapter 29 of postage stamps featuring Diana in her famous gowns.
- Shortly thereafter, another firm advertised the mailing of First Day Covers -- at more than six dollars each -- from different countries that were issuing commemorative postage stamps in honor of Princess Diana.
- Palm Beachers could purchase a Limited Edition Boehm porcelain of "England's Rose" (Chapter 32).
- Multiple ads appeared for Danbury Mint Princess Diana Bride Dolls "in mint condition" -- generally from $600 to $1,000.
- The prompt sale of "official" silver coins commemorating Princess Diana could have been predicted.
- The linkage of "Palm Beach" and "princess" became a natural. A full-page ad appeared in *The Palm Beach Post* on November 7, 1997 announcing a refurnished casino ship operating from the Port of Palm Beach. It now was named "The Palm Beach Princess".

Hairdressers at both walk-in beauty shops and pricy salons also profited from the appeal of Diana's hair styles. Stylists were handed photos and asked to duplicate "the look." Women with medium-to-thick straight hair found it particularly flattering... even without blonde coloring.

The Coincidence of Mother Teresa's Death

The demise of another widely revered women coincided with that of Diana, thereby enhancing pathos internationally. Prior to her death one day before Diana's funeral, Mother Teresa -- the 87-year-old frail nun hailed for her efforts on behalf of the poor, sick, bereaved and dying -- expressed personal sadness over the tragedy that befell the Princess. The Mother was planning to participate in special funeral prayers for Diana, but then succumbed to a terminal heart attack.

Although these women came from totally different social, economic and religious backgrounds, their efforts converged. Photos of the pair during four personal meetings (from 1992 to June 1997) understandably intrigued the world.

Editorials opined that Diana set standards for glamour and fashion, while Mother Teresa set them for compassion and humility. (The nun continued to be dressed in the $1 white habit she wore through her ministry, and in which she accepted the Nobel Peach Prize in 1979.) In the final analysis, however, these remarkable women regarded apathy as unacceptable. By their own examples, they nudged the world to exercise compassionate concern for one another in the face of seemingly insoluble problems.

Steve Gushee, religion editor of *The Palm Beach Post*, wrote that Teresa's death put Diana's life in perspective (September 7, 1997, p. D-8). His column began, "God has a wonderful sense of timing." He sarcastically observed:

> "The *paparazzi* never chased Teresa for a candid shot of her tending the sick. But she won the Nobel Peace Prize in 1979 for her work with the poor. She found in poverty and service a peace that Diana, with wealth and servants, could not attain."[2]

Reflections on a Threatened Monarchy

Death takes no bribes.
Benjamin Franklin *(Poor Richard's Almanac)*

The inhabitants and staff of Buckingham Palace had cold-shouldered Diana in life. But they could not ignore the thick carpet of flowers placed before this and other royal palaces as a tribute by her mourners.

Disdain for the Royal Family

The royal family found it opportune to take Diana back into its fold by arranging a "unique funeral for a unique person" that would be attended by millions on the streets of London -- with or without its invitation. The absence of any statement from the royal family until the eleventh hour, coupled with the decision against allowing Diana's coffin to lie in state, received much criticism both in Britain and abroad.

> Queen Elizabeth II gave her first live television address since 1959 (!) the day before the funeral. She stated, "I admired and respected her... as an exceptional and gifted human being." This statement was designed to diminish the sting of the royal family for having remained distant and aloof so long.

There was another ironic aspect to the timing of Diana's death: the forthcoming 50th Wedding Anniversary of Queen Elizabeth and Prince Philip.

The popularity of Prince Charles plummeted precipitously in Britain and elsewhere. A *Wall Street Journal*-NBC poll of 2,000 persons gave him a public approval rating even lower than House Speaker Newt Gingrich since his budget strategy shut down the federal government (*The Palm Beach Post* September 21, 1997, p. A-2).

Whither the Monarchy?

As Britain experienced a national catharsis, its citizens pondered the monarchy's future. Royal biographer Anthony Holden added this sobering sentiment:

> "She (Diana) was banished by the royal family, but she was the star member of the royal family. It will be hard to see what they will be without her."

In the wake of this singular defining moment, the House of Windsor had to confront a stark reality. As British political institutions were being modernized in a democratic era, the monarchal legacies seemed anachronistic. At stake were reforms involving a formal bill of rights, a weakening of the House of Lords, and elected assemblies in Scotland and Wales.

Yet another shock beset the royal family. It involved the realization that the fate of the British monarchy no longer rested with some Divine Right, but with the willingness of Parliament -- and a hostile Labor Party majority -- to dole out $100 million or more annually to maintain it. Absent such support, its members might have to do something else... such as finding jobs.

Several Palm Beachers already had made tongue-in-cheek suggestions about local opportunities (Chapter 28). Helen Fealy underscored her previous overtures because these "refugees" would "give pizazz to the familiar revolving-door chairladies" (*Palm Beach Daily News* September 17, 1997, p. A-8). She promised that the local cadre of photographers "would never be intrusive." Helen also envisioned the royal emigrants as the Town's ace-in-the-hole should Donald Trump lose interest "in our precious little island."

[1]©1997 *Sun-Sentinel*. Reproduced with permission from the *Sun-Sentinel*, Fort Lauderdale, Florida.
[2]©1997 *The Palm Beach Post*. Reproduced with permission.

31

Personal Reflections: Overlapping Interests and Royal Coincidences

A ministering angel shall my sister be.
Shakespeare
(*Hamlet*)

As, leaving some grand waterfall,
We, lingering, list its roar.
So memory will hallow all
We've known, but know no more.
Abraham Lincoln
(Written at age of 37)

Carol informed me of Diana's death in Orlando shortly after I had given several invitational lectures to a large international conference of physicians and nutritionists. Our reactions duplicated those of millions... but with unique twists.

On returning home, we reflexively pulled out a prized picture of Carol greeting Diana, as I shook hands with Prince Charles, following the couple's arrival at Palm Beach International Airport on a windy November day in 1985 (see Photo Section). Who could have predicted the tragic sight of another flight by Charles -- escorting Diana's coffin back to London?

This tragedy evoked an unexpected response on my part. I had just received the galley proofs of my novel, THE CACOF CONSPIRACY: LESSONS OF THE NEW MILLENNIUM. I nevertheless delayed their final editing in order to complete the present book as a dictate of conscience in Diana's honor, as well as providing much material being sought by her fans.

During this project, I was surprised by the number of themes that overlapped with my own activities and encounters -- besides meetings with Princess Diana and Prince Charles described in earlier chapters. These interests that my wife and I shared with Princess Diana, directly or indirectly, are recounted here, along with some "royal coincidences."

I preface this chapter with repetition of the statement that it was not motivated primarily by ego. Rather, these vignettes emphasize the worldwide scope of humanitarian concerns and efforts being made with others in the tradition of Diana... the vast majority never having been publicized. They became reinforced by insights provided posthumously by Lana Marks, Diana's "American personal friend" (Chapter 32.)

Palm Beach and the Paparazzi

I witnessed the *paparazzi* at every event of the Royal Couple's visit to Palm Beach. Their rude and intrusive tactics were fierce. This caused ALL photographers -- including Palm Beach's finest -- to receive marching orders

103

from security police early in the course of The Breakers banquet (Chapter 20).

These firsthand observations enabled me to understand the anger exhibited by Arnold Schwarzenegger and his wife (Maria Shriver), and the outrage of Alec Baldwin and his wife (Kim Basinger) when they found themselves ambushed by *paparazzi*... literally. I recalled the remark by an equally-harassed Jacqueline Kennedy Onassis to the effect that she no longer belonged to herself.

Charles Spencer forthrightly asserted before his sister's funeral, "I always believed the press would kill her in the end."

Furthermore, security personnel at The Breakers and the local Ritz-Carlton Hotel strictly review and regulate media credentials. Persons who lack them are summarily escorted off the property. The security force employs additional tactics to preclude entry of the *paparazzi*, and adheres to virtual total secrecy about guest lists.

It is axiomatic, however, that the *paparazzi* will continue snooping around Palm Beach. This was evident during the William Kennedy Smith rape trial when photographers regularly staked out Sprinkles Ice Cream & Sandwich Shop at 253 Royal Poinciana Way, a known celebrity haunt.

The Seat Belt Issue

The Charles C Thomas Company published my large text in 1971 titled, THE CAUSES, ECOLOGY AND PREVENTION OF TRAFFIC ACCIDENTS. It emphasized the important role of seat belts in preventing and minimizing serious vehicular injuries.

The world again was forced to consider this issue in the wake of Diana's death and that of two other persons who accompanied her. The sole survivor was the only one wearing a seat belt. For millions of drivers and passengers, this undeniable fact remains the most constructive lesson of the tragedy.

Alcohol and Drug Use by Drivers

In a similar context, I detailed in the aforementioned book the adverse effects of alcohol and many drugs -- both prescription and over-the-counter -- on driver performance. The high blood alcohol concentrations detected on three separate determinations in Henri Paul, driver of the ill-fated Mercedes S-280, reinforced this message. The threat became compounded by his concomitant use of an antidepressant drug (Prozac®) and a tranquilizer.

Spokespersons for The Breakers and its limousine services adamantly affirmed their "zero tolerance" for drinking on the job or drug use of any kind in order to protect patrons (*Palm Beach Daily News* September 4, 1997, p. 2).

The neuropsychiatric effects of another chemical, aspartame (NutraSweet®), will be considered below. They include severe sleepiness, tremors, aberrant behavior, and even convulsions at the wheel of a vehicle or the controls of a plane. (Aspartame originally was developed as a drug for possible use in treating peptic ulcer.)

A Hogarth Etching

The discussion of Anne Boleyn and her death (Chapter 30) triggered a vague déjà vu that I could not identify for a while. The answer crystallized on September 10, 1997, shortly after Diana's funeral, when I gave my daughter Pamela several Hogarth etchings on the occasion of moving into her new home. It suddenly occurred to me that one of his classic works titled, "King Henry the Eighth & Anna Bullen" (see Figure), engraved by J. Cook, had hung in my "gallery" for two decades. Another coincidence surfaced: I purchased it at Harrods, currently owned by the Fayed family.

Engraving of William Hogarth titled:
"King Henry the Eighth & Anna Bullen."
(Author's Collection)

I collected art by William Hogarth (1697-1764), especially his narrative and oft-satiric engravings, because of admiration for their originality, technic and content. Several of his famous suites (e.g., "The Rake's Progress" and "A Harlot's Progress") were purchased from reputable dealers in London's Old Bond Street. I also visited the British Museum to discuss Hogarth's works with one of its acknowledged experts.

Two aspects related to this hobby are noteworthy. First, Hogarth almost singlehandedly championed the copyright law of 1735... still known as the Hogarth Act. Second, the great English painter Constable stated that Hogarth "had never been imitated with tolerable success."

Trauma Care

Some details involving Diana's fatal accident were recounted in Chapter 30. Others deserve mention because of their professional importance to me (see above), and to my wife, Palm Beach County Commissioner Carol A. Roberts.

Stated bluntly, the "golden hour" for possibly saving Diana's life was wasted. This term refers to the first hour after major trauma during which heroic measures are most likely to be effective -- especially stopping major bleeding and performing emergency surgery. In Diana's case, there was a delay of 105 minutes from the arrival of an ambulance to reaching the hospital. Moreover, the ambulance bypassed at least two major hospitals. Deficiencies of the local emergency medical services system involved the absence of an enhanced 9-1-1 phone system, immediate communication with trained medical and paramedical personnel, and proper extrication equipment such as "the Jaws of Life."

Carol had a longstanding commitment to quality trauma care. Indeed, she staked her political career in support of a modest tax to institute major trauma management for the <u>one million</u> inhabitants of Palm Beach County. In response to some infuriated taxpayers, she emphasized that many deaths and permanent injuries could be prevented or minimized by having state-of-the-art facilities. These include an improved 9-1-1 system, trained personnel with proper emergency vehicles and extrication equipment, an emergency helicopter ("Traumahawk"), and two high quality hospital-based trauma centers. Her EMS efforts proved fruitful, and became operational in May 1991... to the gratitude of thousands of subsequent accident victims.

Quasi-Royalty

Citizens of the United States are not supposed to kneel before royalty. After all, isn't that how the country got started?

On the basis of first-hand observations, I find that most Americans are bowled over by visiting royalty. The impact tends to be proportionate to the degree of royal blood and the thickness of one's accent. It also extends to some American women who married into royal families. As a result, they could legitimately tack on "Duchess" or "Princess" to their names (e.g., Princess Grace of Monaco).

The closest home-grown facsimiles to royalty are elected officials and movie stars. One might think that persons orbiting in high socioeconomic spheres would be relatively immune to such reverential behavior. But the introduction of Carol Roberts with prefixes such as "The Honorable," "Commissioner," or "Mayor" almost predictably made sophisticated Palm Beachers take notice.

This matter assumed even more robust proportions when Carol went on official state and charitable visits abroad -- such as being the official United States observer for the first democratic elections held in Latvia and Estonia. During several humanitarian visits to East Africa countries as the President of Assisting Communities Toward Self-Help, Mayor Carol Roberts was addressed as "Your Worship." This "title" never failed to amuse her and her entourage of political and business leaders.

Many notable persons holding high political office in Britain and elsewhere also accorded Carol respect. One such meeting was with former Prime Minister Margaret Thatcher (see Photo Section).

Doctoring "Blue Bloods"

I doctored many Palm Beachers for over four decades. A number of unusual encounters with persons from high socioeconomic brackets who reside on the island are described in my recent book, HEALTH AND WEALTH, PALM BEACH STYLE.

As with visiting royalty, ordinary folk often refer to such individuals as having "blue blood." A practising physician, however, may be confronted with the literal use of this term in a literal sense.

A prominent socialite had been under my care many years. He developed progressive anemia from intermittent bleeding due to a hiatus hernia, and ultimately required transfusions. Feeling energized after receiving his second transfusion, he joked, "I lost my blue blood and now have red blood!"

Reflections on a Quick-Change Artist

Princess Diana's frequent changes of wardrobe (Chapter 29) struck a responsive note concerning my own wife. Her schedule became increasingly packed, especially while serving as the Mayor of West Palm Beach and then as Chair of the Palm Beach County Commission. Carol would have to flit from one "politically required" meeting to another... and even another. These appearances necessitated logistic arrangements regarding dress.

The sandwiching of "wardrobe incompatible" events, especially on weekends, proved a specially daunting challenge. For example, Carol was scheduled to offer "Greetings" to the Tri-County National Business League Luncheon at the Royce Hotel at 1 PM on Saturday, October 24, 1987. An appearance for the informal Farmfest at 2:30 PM followed, and then a semi-formal event at the Executive Club. She solved the problem in two ways: carrying enough clothes for two changes, and then making a mad dash home for the evening transformation.

One happy beneficiary of such frequent quick changes was our dry clothes cleaner.

The Touch of Royalty, Cinema Style:

A Reel Coincidence

The Carefree Theatre in West Palm Beach exhibited large posters that advertised its feature full-length attraction, *Scooter in Palm Beach*, the first week of April 1988. (It could not be shown in The Town of Palm Beach, which no longer has public movie theatres by decree.) The poster showed a formal dinner scene in a Palm Beach mansion. The hostess, played by Carol Roberts, sat at the end of the table (see Photo Section). She portrayed a Palm Beach socialite entertaining "The Prince and The Princess" in this fictional script. There were three intriguing -- and pertinent -- lines under this photo:

> *The Prince and the Princess are in town...*
> *Scooter is on the loose...*
> *Palm Beach will never be the same...*

The movie centered about an 8-year-old boy and his misadventures on the island. This independent production by Paul V. Dillow was directed by Marlene Rogoff.

The film premiered simultaneously on March 31, 1988 in West Palm Beach and Los Angeles. The initial performance locally benefitted two of Carol's favorite charities -- Assisting Communities Toward Self-Help (ACTS) and Cities in Schools (an anti-dropout program). Rogoff said of Palm Beach County Commissioner Chairman Carol Roberts: "In a way, she is the most well-known (actor). It was wonderful of her to donate her time. I enjoyed very much working with her" (*The Palm Beach Post* March 10, 1988).

A full house saw the first local performance. The audience included many friends who sought to honor Carol by donating to her favorite charities -- at $100 per person. Carol was introduced and presented with a large bouquet of roses.

But others came to see the movie. This was evidenced by a long line of customers standing for a second non-benefit showing the same evening.

The reporters who covered this extraordinary story, involving the Chair of the Palm Beach County Commission, had a field day. Their features appeared on the front pages of local news sections on P(premiere)-Day. *The Palm Beach Post* (March 31, 1988, p. D-1) displayed the cited photo in color of Carol, as Mrs. Ratskill, hosting a formal party for royalty.

Some of Carol's colleagues in government and politics found themselves caught up in the action. The press kept hounding her at meetings and restaurants -- even prior to the P-Day. In fact, her dinner at the Executive Club was interrupted twice by the head waiter who felt obliged to inform her about a related "urgent phone call."

Intrigue was heightened by the following poem in the invitation to the premiere.

> *Right here at home... a star is born,*
> *Our County Chairman's career is torn,*
> *She has the lead in this premiere show,*
> *Which career wins out we will soon know.*
>
> *Now you're invited to this review,*
> *"Scooter in Palm Beach"... it's brand new.*
> *The theater place is the "CAREFREE"...*
> *Come see the show as a V.I.P.*

The media were especially curious as to how Carol happened to be offered the leading role. Hundreds of women had unsuccessfully auditioned for this part before a somewhat reluctant Carol agreed to read several lines of the script... all the while thinking "audition" was a big joke concocted by her brother. Director Marlene Rogoff, told *The Miami Herald* that Carol was selected "...because she has a natural sense for comedy... I thought she was best for the part" (March 31, 1988, p. C-3).

When queried about the most challenging aspect of this role, Carol fessed up: having a bowl of pea soup dumped over her.

Carol had some reservations about this "kids' film" that disparaged pretentiousness in and around Palm Beach -- ranging from irresponsible spending for art on Worth Avenue to polo. She clarified for *The Miami Herald* that the dizzy socialite she portrayed "...doesn't reflect me." Carol added, "My character, Mrs. Ratskill, comes to Palm Beach wanting to make it, but she will never make it in Palm Beach society. She doesn't have the grace, the background, and the whole demeanor to fit into the Palm Beach scene."

I had several interesting subsequent encounters with patients. They were duly impressed with the "touch of royalty" conferred upon me by being married to a "movie star" who had previously hosted Prince Charles and Princess Diana.

My waiting room on Monday morning, April 4, held an interesting mix of patients. One who had grown up in the "East Side" of New York had all the mannerisms of this genre. The others owned two residences -- one on Park Avenue in New York; and the other in a prestigious Palm Beach apartment house. The lady hailing from the less affluent area of the Big Apple stated on entering my office: "It was interesting to hear your patients who live on Park Avenue." When the Palm Beach couple entered, their first words were: "How does it feel to be married to a famous movie star, Doctor?"

Over the ensuing years, Carol kept hearing that *Scooter* was still shown all over the world, including London. Audiences were intrigued by her acting, and by the beauty of Palm Beach and local affluent communities, especially their lovely homes.

A subsequent revelation also linked Diana to the film industry. She had expressed interest in a movie co-starring with Kevin Costner for a sequel to *The Bodyguard*. After discussions for over a year, Costner received the second draft three days before Diana died... the plot being loosely based on her life. Costner would play the bodyguard with whom she fell in love. He praised the script as "dignified, sexy, smart and funny" (*The Miami Herald,* November 19, 1997, p. A-7).

AIDS Assistance by Commissioner

Carol Roberts

Profound concern over AIDS victims aligned the sympathies and independent activities of Princess Diana and my wife. Carol's persistent efforts at the local level became critical.

Mention was made of directing the proceeds raised at the premiere of *Scooter in Palm Beach* to AIDS-related activities. Several weeks earlier, *The Palm Beach Post* (March 14, 1988, p. 4) stated, "Palm Beach County Commission Chairman Carol Roberts helped establish the new 24-bed AIDS unit at the county home on 45th Street."

I regretted the death of Diana before her planned return to Palm Beach for a related reason: the opportunity for the Princess and Carol to share their ongoing altruistic efforts and future projects. Along with many others, I would have liked to be a fly on the nearby wall overhearing this conversation.

The Aspartame (NutraSweet®) Issue

I experienced another one-of-a-kind personal reaction. Mention was made of Diana's depression, anorexia and bulimia (forced vomiting) in Chapter 30. For over a decade, I had been describing the serious effects of aspartame (NutraSweet®) products -- especially among women with depression, other psychiatric problems, and weight-related disorders (bulimia; anorexia; obesity). The details appear in three books on Aspartame Disease (a term I coined)[1,2,3] and more than a score of original articles and letters, many in peer-reviewed publications.

The reader can imagine my response on seeing a can of Diet Coke© next to Diana in a *The New York Times* photo (September 9, 1997, Section 4, p. 5)! Considering the depression and eating affliction of this weight- and figure-conscious supermodel, I suspected that these problems could have been aggravated by her use of aspartame products -- an opinion based on more than 1,100 aspartame reactors in my data base.

More on the "Fear of Fat"

The "fear of fat" -- a term I used in several books discussing the present epidemic of anorexia and bulima -- also had afflicted her sister Sarah. By coincidence, the same psychiatrist (Dr. Maurice Lipsedge) who treated Sarah in the late 1970s later attended Diana for bulimia. She would make herself vomit as many as five times a day! (Diana was found devouring a bag of sweets or food from the refrigerator on several occasions.)

The indifference and rejection by Charles influenced such behavior. It is illustrated by several vignettes.

- Before her wedding day, he commented that Diana's figure was "chubby" after putting his arm around her waist.
- While sick during a visit with Spain's royal family, Charles wondered aloud why Diana couldn't be "more like Fergie."

Diana instinctively knew that the cure for her eating disorder resided in affection and patience from Charles and her in-laws, and cessation of "malice in the palace" -- not the psychoactive drugs or diets doctors recommended. She felt even more convinced after correlating her problem with trying visits to the royal family at their various abodes. This conclusion seemed conclusive after considerable reading on the matter, and finding that many others suffered with similar afflictions. Diana finally experienced much relief after baring her pent-up emotions and frustrations to trusted friends and physicians.

A Dianasque Role

Diana's involvement in many causes were repeatedly mentioned. They became increasingly meaningful because of my ongoing activities aimed at banning aspartame as an "imminent public health hazard." These efforts were totally corporate- and institutional-neutral... meaning I had received no grants or money for them.

I was later joined by scores of concerned persons from dozens of countries in criticizing aspartame manufacturers, distributors and "sciencegate" researchers, along with apathetic regulatory agencies worldwide that had permitted this perceived travesty. (As a case in point, over half of adults in the United States currently consume aspartame products.) Unbeknown to me at first, and with no personal input, these volunteers began calling themselves "Roberts Angels." I initially disavowed the term on the grounds it might be used by critics to infer egomania.

In my heart of hearts, I felt that Diana would have been pleased with this nutritional and ecologic effort that had now assumed international proportions. Unfortunately, I had no tangible evidence of her aspartame consumption while still alive in order to provide a "curbstone consultation" that might have been beneficial.

A Distaste for Fancy Cars

I was impressed by another evidence of Diana's sensitivity for persons suffering economic hardship: her insistence upon using a "pool" car owned by Buckingham Palace rather than being chauffeured in an ostentatious private vehicle.

This attitude had a unique effect on me. I had refused to buy or rent <u>any</u> luxury car throughout my years of practice on the premise that its presence in my parking area would offend poor patients seeing "the doctor's fancy auto."

A Plea for Professional Tolerance

The reader recognizes my admiration for Princess Diana as a larger-than-life public figure who attempted to do much good. Out of both respect and professional limitations, I have delayed discussing one issue alluded to by critics of Diana: her psychological status and stability.

Having had half a century experience dealing with troubled patients and families, I always try to remain objective in such matters. There often <u>are</u> two (or more) sides to interpersonal problems, particularly private conflicts that culminate in divorce.

Warped Psychologic Inferences

A number of psychologic allegations about Diana were made posthumously. Examples of inferences about this version of the "psychic bloodline of the royal family" included terms such as "the goddess of troubled women," "the goddess of bulima," and characterization of her death as "a sublimated sexual assault" (*The Palm Beach Post* September 28, 1997, p. B-1). Diana's admission to having contemplated suicide as many as five times on direct questioning by an eating-disorder specialist had been publicized.

Some underscored Diana's psychotrauma during early childhood.

- She was born the third daughter of 37-year-old Viscount Althorp and 25-year-old Viscountess Althorp on July 1, 1961. Her father had hoped for a son to continue the Spencer name -- especially after the death of a badly deformed son shortly after birth 18 months earlier. Diana felt a lingering sense of both disappointment and guilt.
- A related incident figured in such "devaluation." Whereas younger brother Charles was christened with all the pomp at Westminster Abbey, she had been christened in a Sandringham church... commoners serving as godparents.
- A lonely Cinderella-like family existence in later years compounded her anxiety.

Praise For Personal Courage and The Will to Help

As I reflected on Diana's praiseworthy comeback from severe depression, her eating disorders and contemplated suicide, I was reminded of the central character of *The Razor's Edge* (1944) by Somerset Maugham (also a physician). This American war veteran had regained his confidence and ability to help others through deep reflection and spiritual guidance.

Diana did so -- and regained her "smothered" personality -- through counseling, the study of holistic philosophy, reading books such as *The Prophet* by Khahil Gibran, and inspired choral works. She resisted being entombed in abstraction by the royal family by becoming a foxy fighter to regain herself.

In the wake of this reevaluation of values, the attendance of ballets (which she loved), playing the role of a sexy mannequin, and being present at the Ascot parade of fashion came to seem frivolous. Their appeal lessened compared to the difficult personal challenge of giving hope and comfort at hostels for the homeless, sexually abused and terminally-ill, going to hospitals and addiction centers for teenagers with alcoholism and drug abuse, visiting persons afflicted with AIDS and leprosy, and supporting the victims of land mines.

These remarkable constructive attributes had been forged early in life, undoubtedly influenced by the foregoing experiences during childhood. Indeed, Diana evidenced an instinctive affinity and rapport with hyperactive teenagers as a schoolgirl during voluntary visits to a mental hospital.

A Plea for Restraint

Others can argue about Diana's alleged narcissistic personality, her supposed neurotic exploitation to gain sympathy or revenge, and the emotionally-driven compulsion to touch others. On the other hand, her candor without acrimony, her vulnerability, her crushing loneliness, her struggle to regain control, and the deep feeling she eloquently expressed about a ruined marriage during a famous television interview enhanced her emotional bonding with the people... as in "The People's Princess."

I am content to conclude that Diana's outreach to enable humanity in order to ennoble her own dysfunctional life has honorable validity. It is my hope that colleagues will refuse to cheapen the outstanding legacy of her good deeds and intentions with negative armchair aspersions.

[1]Roberts, H.J.: *Aspartame (NutraSweet®): Is It Safe?* Philadelphia, The Charles Press, 1989.
[2]Roberts, H.J.: *Sweet'ner Dearest: Bittersweet Vignettes About Aspartame (NutraSweet®)*. West Palm Beach, Sunshine Sentinel Press, 1992.
[3]Roberts, H.J.: *Defense Against Alzheimer's Disease: A Rational Blueprint for Prevention*. West Palm Beach, Sunshine Sentinel Press, 1995.

32

Farewells to Diana by Palm Beach

Beauty is the mark God sets upon virtue.
Ralph Waldo Emerson
(*Beauty*) (1849)

The heart has its reasons which reason knows nothing of.
Blaise Pascal

Close friends, casual acquaintances and distant admirers of Princess Diana in the Palm Beach area joined to mourn her death. I was impressed by the sincerity of such personal homage by a community with a reputation for ho-humming the visits of American presidents and visiting royalty.

- Palm Beacher Lana Marks, a special friend of Diana (see below), departed for London to attend her funeral. She stated before leaving that the princess had agreed to head a major fund-raiser in March 1998 (*Palm Beach Daily News* September 4, 1997, p. 3).
- Bill Brooks, general manager of TV Channel 5 and a Palm Beach resident, commented that Diana's critical attribute was "her absolutely engaging presence... She was young and beautiful and modern and refreshing" (*Palm Beach Daily News* September 4, 1997, p. 3).
- Celia Lipton Farris, a London-bred resident of Palm Beach and outstanding philanthropist, felt the need to "keep a stiff upper lip. But I'm so sad. My heart goes out to those children. She was becoming a truly great woman" (*Palm Beach Daily News* September 4, 1997, p. 3).

The Episcopal Church of Bethesda-by-the-Sea held a memorial service for Diana, described below, the following week. It resulted from many requests to the British-American Chamber of Commerce, a local business group. A condolence book was available for signing.

Similar activities reflecting affection for Diana occurred in Palm Beach.

- The British Emporium at The Esplanade on Worth Avenue also provided a condolence book. One Palm Beacher stated, "I thought that my words could give comfort to whomever in the family would read this" (*Palm Beach Daily News* September 7, 1997, p. 1).
- Local bookstores and the Main Street News were besieged for magazines and newspapers about Diana's death, and books about her.
- There was a frenzy for the CD of Elton John's remake of *Candle in the Wind* (Chapter 30) on both sides of the lake, the proceeds directed to Diana's favorite charities.

Reflections by the *Palm Beach Daily News*

"The Shiny Sheet" gave much thought to coverage of Diana's death by the news media, including the tactics of *paparazzi.* Considering the many high-profile celebrities who live in or visit the community, and the ever-present corps of Palm Beach photographers (Chapter 20), this theme had struck close to home. Part of its editorial on September 7, 1997 (p. A-8) warrants repetition.

"Although the *Palm Beach Daily News*, like most mainstream media, has no use for the tactics or photographs of the paparazzi, we were nonetheless troubled by the mad rush to assign blame for the tragic deaths in Paris to any segment of the news media. Even more disturbing are the hypocritical calls by some celebrities, in the wake of the accident, for additional legal curbs on news photography...

"The mainstream media also cover celebrity news and occasionally print stories and photographs they would not have produced themselves but that have moved up the 'media food chain' from the tabloids. A certain interest in celebrities is natural, but both society and the media must draw the line between normal and obsessive interest. The latter is what produces the abuses of the paparazzi...

"Efforts by celebrities to muzzle any part of the media are particularly offensive because the stars do not want the media to leave them alone -- that would be fatal to their careers. They just want to control coverage of themselves, limiting it to suit their purposes and convenience. They want the benefits of media attention without the burdens.

"Of course, the paparazzi sometimes go too far, invading the privacy even the most public of personalities deserve. When the paparazzi violate the law or infringe on someone's rights in a way that gives rise to a civil action, they deserve no special protection. But as long as so many of us feel compelled to look at what they produce, we are hardly in a position to condemn them."[1]

Negative Feedback

Although the U.S. Senate declared the Saturday of September 6 as a "National Day of Recognition for the humanitarian efforts of Diana, Princess of Wales," a few Anglophiles expressed negative attitudes about some aspects of the foregoing events.

Raymond B. Knudsen opined: "The earl's attack on the royal family was both out of place and uncalled for..." (*The Palm Beach Post* September 10, 1997, p. A-11). He added: "In Palm Beach County, there are probably a thousand women who are as pretty, as generous and as dedicated to humanitarian services. Without the linchpin of royalty, they do not gain the praise or recognition they deserve."

A few even suggested that Diana's heirs should demand a refund from the "psychics" who had given her incorrect or inadequate advice -- most significantly, not revealing her demise two weeks later.

Although infamous because it was printed just prior to the death, *The Globe* carried this headline relative to Diana's swimsuits, "To Di For!"

The Memorial Service in Palm Beach

Many Palm Beachers and friends residing in nearby communities requested a special service to memorialize Princess Diana. The Episcopal Church of Bethesda-by-the Sea provided this opportunity on September 13, 1997 patterned after the Westminster Abbey service (Chapter 30). It began at 4 PM, and included most of the same readings and hymns -- 1 *Corinthians* 13 (read by David Setford), the two poetic excerpts recited by Diana's sisters, and the hymns *The King of Love* and *Guide Me, O Thou Great Jehovah.*

Bethesda-by-the-Sea is a magnificent structure. First-time visitors tend to be awed by its spiring stone arches, Flemish tapestries of a medieval-like cloister, and its 15th Century stained glass windows.

The Reverend Ralph R. Warren, Jr., Rector of the Church, conducted this 45-minute service. It was attended by about 250 persons who wore wide-brimmed hats and dark suits. Most signed the guest registry.

Unfortunately, the church had sustained a major lightning strike the previous day. This "act of God" disabled its fine organ and tower bells, as well as much of the sound system.

The following prayer for Princess Diana's life and work was recited.

> "The Princess will be especially missed by the many charities with which she identified herself. We recall those precious images: the affectionate cuddle of children in hospitals; that touch of the young man dying of AIDS; her compassion for those maimed through the evil of land mines; and many more.
>
> "LORD we pray for all who are weak, poor and powerless in this country and throughout the world; the sick, among them Trevor Rees-Jones; the maimed and all whose lives are damaged. We thank you for the way that Diana became a beacon of hope and a source of strength for so many. We commend to you all those charities that she supported. Strengthen the resolve of those who work for them to continue the good work begun with her."

Robert Spencer, a second cousin of Diana who winters in Palm Beach (see Photo Section), gave a eulogy. He remembered her in these terms:

> "Someone who performed her different public duties with such skill: at night in gorgeous gowns and dazzling jewels, her chick, her style and effervescent personality excited kings, queens, presidents and first ladies. The next day in a simple attire and a soft smile, she visited sick children and victims of AIDS."

"England's Rose" on Worth Avenue

A large ad by the prestigious firm of Douglas Lori, Inc. on Worth Avenue appeared in the September 21, 1997 edition of *The Palm Beach Post* (p. A-18). It announced a Boehm porcelain sculpture "created in loving memory of Princess Diana 1961-1977." "English's Rose" featured a rose in pristine white, adorned with a coronet of gold. It measured 7 inches wide by 6 inches deep, and sold for $350 -- ten percent of the proceeds being earmarked for the Princess Diana Foundation.

Helen Boehm, owner of the porcelain firm, had been an admirer of Diana. The exquisite gown that she wore at The Ball is described in Chapter 19.

Lana Marks: Diana's "Personal Friend"

Lana Marks, the Palm Beach designer of Diana's handbags and other accessories, has been mentioned several times.

- The Princess greeted Lana shortly after Diana arrived at the New York reception honoring her prior to the auction of her famous gowns two days later (Chapter 29).
- Diana and Lana had been planning a gala fund-raiser at The Breakers Hotel during February 1998 (Chapter 30).
- Marks was invited by the family to attend Diana's funeral at Westminster Abbey (Chapter 30).

The Friendship

The origins and extent of this close friendship between Princess Diana and the local designer intrigued me. Although harboring some understandable reservations in an era characterized by widespread distrust of promotional hype and media reporting, their relationship seemed authentic.

I met Lana Marks at her "first and only" talk about this unique friendship on September 20. A representative of the Barnes & Noble book store in Palm Beach Gardens invited me. The store stocked my history of the Greater West Palm Beach area titled, WEST PALM BEACH: CENTENNIAL REFLECTIONS (Sunshine Sentinel Press). This book included a summary of the 1985 visit by the Royal Couple, along with photos of the associated events.

More on Lana Marks

Despite the foregoing reservations, I found myself enthralled both by Lana's quiet charm and her presentation in a delightful English accent. This "personal perspective" provided many generalities about the relationship. Lana preambled her remarks, however, with the absolute assertion that "my lips are sealed forever" about many private aspects the two had discussed... "even though I might be bursting at the seams (to reveal them)." It was an affirmation of the oath of confidentiality she had given Diana.

I happened to sit next to Lana's family. She was the wife of a psychiatrist-colleague, and the mother of two handsome children -- a 15-year-old son, and a 12-year-old daughter.

Lana's reputation as a fine designer of handbags (Lana of London) already had been established before the Princess contacted her. Her work appeared in *Vogue* Magazine, and was sold by major fashion stores (e.g., Bergdorff Goodman).

The Princess was pleased by the "fashionable and functional" handbag that Lana designed. (It represented considerable research.) Diana then requested more bags in a variety of colors, especially neutral shades. These generated further appreciation of Lana's talent. Orders for other items followed, such as special belts for Diana's trips to Africa and elsewhere. They also became favorites of Diana because of their originality and appropriateness.

"A Personal Friend"

Lana could not understand why she was being bombarded by influential persons with non-business questions. The answer was forthcoming with this question posed by Lucia Flecha de Lima, the wife of Brazil's Ambassador in Washington: "Would you consider becoming a personal and confidential friend of Princess Diana?"

She felt overwhelmed by this Cinderella-like proposition. Lana gave an affirmative answer -- but all the while thinking, "Why me? I'm just an ordinary person!"

The "Game of Phone Tag"

Diana and Lana conversed at least three times weekly... often several times a day. Each call lasted 45 minutes or longer. There was a pre-arranged pattern. Diana would ring Lana. After identifying herself, she hung up, and promptly called on a portable phone with a scrambler to ensure privacy. (Diana learned that her telephone calls at Kensington Palace had been "bugged" with listening devices!)

This arrangement led to several humorous incidents.

- The secretary of Lana's husband assumed that the person "calling herself Princess Diana" had to be one of his psychiatric patients.
- A guest staying at the same London hotel patronized by Lana was dialed inadvertently. Assuming the "royal caller" to be a prankster, she promptly put down the receiver.

As a perceptive and experienced businesswoman, Lana could size up most individuals. Accordingly, I was moved by the positive terms she used to describe Diana's consistent attributes -- "sweet"; "gracious"; "kind"; "affectionate"; "hilarious sense of humor"; "extremely prompt"; "well organized"; "highly considerate"; "elegant"; and of course "very beautiful." They are illustrated by these anecdotes.

- Diana served (and drank) coffee -- instead of tea -- when she invited Lana to lunch at Kensington Palace. This reflected respect for a friend from the United States where coffee was the national beverage.
- Diana carefully noted how her guests from different nations used cutlery, and followed suit to put them at ease.
- The two women repeatedly roared with laughter over many topics, largely generated by Diana's great sense of humor. Few subjects were off limits in their secret tête-a-tête sessions.
- Diana escorted Lana to her cab after their first luncheon at Kensington Palace. The guest recalled the amazement of the driver with whom the Princess chatted, and her <u>insistence</u> upon opening the door for Lana by herself.

Lana reciprocated by going to extremes to protect these confidential discussions and meetings, especially during visits to London. She nearly panicked when Diana requested that <u>Lana</u> pick the venue for their next luncheon in February 1997.

Lana ultimately decided upon the atrium of the restaurant in the fine hotel she frequented while in London. Her demands about <u>major</u> security, <u>total</u> absence of the press, and a special cuisine focused on Diana's favorites were unconditional -- and fully met. Indeed, the manager did not inform his own staff of the visit by the Princess until 30 minutes before her prompt arrival at 1 PM.

Reflections On Having a "Personal Friend"

The author's appreciation of the importance that prominent women attach to having a "special female friend" is relevant. My remarkable wife provides a case in point.

Carol Roberts is a well-known local leader and elected official -- four-term Commissioner of West Palm Beach and its Mayor; three-term Commissioner and Chair of the Palm Beach County Commission -- with boundless energy. She is also respected nationally and internationally for her knowledge of (and involvement in) government, transportation, housing, education, health care and relief work. For good measure, this beautiful and fashionable woman is highly photogenic... therefore a photographer's delight.

When thorny issues involving various matters arose, Carol could confide her feelings to Anita Mitchell -- and vice versa. This charming and brilliant person had experienced a lifetime of bitter challenges and rib-tickling encounters that could fill a large book. (She had been married to Ed Mitchell, the astronaut.) Although coming from totally different family, professional, religious and political backgrounds, Carol and Anita forged a cherished friendship. This included making themselves available to one another on a 24-hour basis when urgent matters requiring input or catharsis developed. Recognizing the obvious instinctive and constructive need for such female dialogue, I felt neither slighted nor ignored.

Returning to the isolated and later-divorced Diana, I could easily fathom her intense desire for a trustworthy confidante. As a corollary, I assumed that Lana's psychiatrist-husband sympathized with the Diana-Lana link in a similar manner.

> Mention was made about the intrigue over "How does a handbag designer come to be Diana's close friend?" Various persons expressed their theories to me. One couple felt that it represented a subterfuge to hide the supposition that Dr. Marks had been the key member of the family as Diana's alleged psychiatrist!

The Boys

Lana confirmed that Diana's sons, William and Harry, constituted her top priority. She adored the boys, constantly talking about them with Lana. Diana routinely canceled <u>all</u> appointments when they returned from Eton or elsewhere.

Diana's love for her sons, and devoted concern over their proper and humanistic upbringing, became unequivocal to Lana. When they were home, she often heard them laughing or giggling in the background while chatting with Diana.

As noted, Lana's own children were the same ages. She accordingly used them as resource persons to decide on "neat" gifts for Diana's sons. Tiffany's suggestion about Palm Beach sweat shirts proved right on target.

Diana and her sons often watched videos together. She joked to Lana, "We are the Kensington couch potatoes."

> One pearl emerged. Diana's favorite actress was Goldie Hawn. In point of fact, Lana had been planning a surprise appearance by Goldie at the forthcoming Palm Beach fund-raiser.

Lana conveyed Diana's passionate desire to have William and Harry see "the real world." They would sneak out "the back door" of Kensington Palace to visit hospitals, hospices and homeless shelters. Lana emphasized that for every such publicized visit, ten other unheralded ones were not reported.

> A funny story involved such a surprise nocturnal visit by Diana. A hospitalized patient told his doctor one morning that he probably needed more medicine. Why? He thought he was hallucinating about "a visit from Princess Diana last night."

More Vignettes

Lana Marks provided additional insights about Diana's sense of good fortune in having found a trustworthy close friend.

- Lana kept using the word "outstanding" when she commented on Diana's all-around exquisite taste. The Princess replied, "You've given me new meaning for that word."
- Diana often asked for affirmation on some point. She repeated the expression, "Do you really think so?"
- Disregarding all others, the Princess would embrace Lana on meeting her at various functions.

Diana felt the need for trusted input while visiting the United States. She therefore demanded that Lana be invited to ALL American events. This would ensure a respected opinion on the spot.

There was one notable response in the negative. It occurred during the reception before her gowns were auctioned (Chapter 29). When Diana asked Lana if she planned to buy one, she replied, "I really don't have that much money!"

Concerning the subject of handbags, I hesitated to ask this authority the question, "What in the world does Queen Elizabeth carry in her bag? After all, why would she need a photo ID, or credit cards, or even a small gun for protection?" But I held my tongue. There had been enough embarrassment over captions such as, "Charles wears the skirt, but his mother carries the purse" (*The Miami Herald* September 20, 1997, p. A-11).

After being introduced by her husband, I showed Lana the photo in WEST PALM BEACH: CENTENNIAL REFLECTIONS of Carol greeting Princess Diana during her 1985 visit. Visibly impressed by such documentation, and this heretofore-unknown account of the visit, I presented Lana with the volume... autographing it for good measure.

Lana closed by relating a poignant experience that had a lasting effect. Prince William sat directly opposite her during the service at Westminster Abbey. This enabled Lana to observe the lad closely... especially his "body language." She repeatedly kept telling herself, "Why, that's Diana!" Lana then offered this prediction: "King William will be one of the greatest English kings because of his Mother's loving care and influence!"

Permanent Memorials

The Palm Beach Branch of the Order of St. John Hospitaller and Order of St. George had a unique interest in the death of Princess Diana. As the venerable head of the Order of Knights Hospitaller, Queen Elizabeth received this message from Palm Beach Knights and Dames of Malta.

H.M. Queen Elizabeth II

Please accept our heartfelt condolences
on the tragic death of
Diana, Princess of Wales.
She attained heroic virtue as the
beautiful and beloved champion of
charitable causes,
and shall be sorely missed.
We salute her here on earth as
the angels receive her in heaven.

This reply from Balmoral Castle shortly followed.

"The Queen, The Prince of Wales, Prince William and Prince Harry, and all the members of the family are most grateful for your thoughtful expression of sympathy on the sudden and tragic death of Diana, Princess of Wales."

"The Private Secretary has been asked to thank you for your kindness in writing as you did at such a sad time."

The Palm Beach Knights and Dames of Malta donated to the placement of Maltese Crosses as memorials to Princess Diana at the site of her accident, the hospital where she died, and the chapel. This was in the tradition of a tribute by Edward I (reign from 1272-1307) to Queen Eleanor. Crosses were erected on each of the twelve sites where her coffin rested during the funeral procession to Westminster Abbey. Charing Cross, often regarded as the heart of London, took its name from one of these memorials.

[1]©1997 *Palm Beach Daily News*. Reproduced with permission.

A

Abdication Desk 8
Adams, Ken 40, 44
Addison, Stayton 55
adverse effects of alcohol 104
AIDS 92, 108, 110
al-Fayed, Mohamed 8, 97
Albritton, Joe 54
Althorp 98
Ambassador Arthur Gardner 5
Ambassador E. T. Smith 11
American Communist Party 12
American Friends of the Black Rose 76
Anglophiles 42, 83
Anglophiles of Palm Beach 18
anorexia 96, 108
Anti-Defamation League 12
Appleman, Ann 78
Arm & Hammer 68
Armand Hammer Collection 25
Armand Hammer United World College of
    the American West 22
Army Major James Hewitt 84
arrival 41
asparagus 55
aspartame 104, 108
aspartame disease 108
Assisting Communities Toward Self-Help
    (ACTS) 27, 107
auction 89
Avis, Warren Edward 27, 54

B

Baldwin, Alec 104
Bardot, Brigitte 94
Barrantes, Susan 79
Barry, Dave 14
battered women 92
Beane, Geoffrey 52
Berger, David 80
Bernstein-Fealy, Helen 87, 102
Berry, Wendy 82
Bethesda-by-the-Sea 111
Blum, Maitresse 8
Boehm, Helen 53, 55, 92, 113
Boehm porcelain sculpture 113
Boleyn, Anne 94, 104
Borge, Victor 9, 56
Bowles, Camilla Parker 83, 97
Brando, Marlon 94
Breakers Hotel, The 2, 49, 50
Britannia 77, 78
British fashion industry 84
British history 37
British lineage of American presidents 70
British nobility 35
Brooks, William 63, 111
Brown, Edmund G. 54
Bryan, John 86
Buchwald, Art 70
Buckingham Palace 9, 62, 82, 98, 102
bulimia 83, 96, 108
Burke's Peerage 84
Butler Aviation Terminal 40

C

cameras 31
cancer 92
Candle In the Wind 99
Carling, Will 84
Cartland, Barbara 37, 97
Christie's 89
Churchill, Winston 6
Cinderella 50, 56, 96
Cities in Schools 107
Clinton, Hillary 76
clothes 88
coffin 98
Collins, Joan 9, 54, 55
Colony Hotel 5
communism 11
Community Chest 11
compassion 96
Complete Guide to Executive Manners 38
controversy 10
correspondence 62
Crichton, Alexander William 4
critics 15
Cromwell, Oliver 20, 37
Cronholm, Anna 75
Cummings, Alan 11
Curb, Mike 54
curtseying 31

D

D.C. visit 9
Dalai Lama 67
Dear Abby 9
Death of Princess Diana 91
delayed Bar Mitzvah 68
depression 83, 96, 108
Di-vestment by a Fashion Icon 88
Diana in private 83
Diana's funeral 97
Diana's psychotrauma during early
    childhood 110
"Diana's rainbow coalition," 98
diet sodas 52
discourtesy 18
distaste for fancy cars 109
divorce 84
Dodge, Gregg 16
Dole, Bob 70
Donahue, Jimmy 5
Donahue, Mary Woolworth 16
Donahues 5
Douglas Lori, Inc. 113
Douthit, Nancy 10
Dr. and Mrs. Henri Kayzer-Andre 55
Drexel, Noreen 46
drugs 104
du Pont, Bunny and Nicky 5
Duchess 8
Duchess of Windsor 6
Duchess of York 79
Dudley, Guilford 54
Dudley, Jane 46
Duke and Duchess of Windsor 5, 38, 100
Duke of Windsor 5, 35

Dunphy, Chris 5
"dysfunctional" 81
dysfunctional family 96

E

E.R. Bradley's Saloon 16
Earl Spencer 99
eating disorders 96
Economic boost 46
Edelstein, Victor 89
Edward I 117
Elizabeth II 86
Emporium, British at The Esplanade 111
"England's Rose" 100, 113
English monarchy 35
English-Speaking Union of Palm Beach 3
entrepreneurs 101
envelope 22
epic grief 98
Epicurean Restaurant 46
Epstein, Edward Jay 66
etiquette 73
Everglades Club 5
Everywoman 100
Everywoman touch 94

F

Fairbanks, Douglas 79
Farewells 111
Farris, Celia Lipton 18, 53, 55, 78, 111
Fashion Princess 38
fatal accident 105
Faustian bargain 94
Fayed, Dodi 93, 97
Fealy, Helen 87, 102
"Fear of Fat" 109
Fergie: Her Secret Life 86
Ferguson, Sarah 79, 86, 100
First Battalion Welsh guards 98
first day covers 101
first husbands club 85
flowers 20, 97
Fomon, Bob and Lewis 79
Forbes, Malcolm 9, 54
Founding Fathers 3
"friendship ring" 93

G

Gabor, Eva 44, 54
"Game of Phone Tag" 114
Gardiner, Eunice 46
Gardner, Arthur 5
Getty, Ann 75
Gilet, Eles 90
Glisson, Bink 44
Goldsmith, Christina de Caraman 79
Good Samaritan Hospital 8, 61
Goodbye, England's Rose 99
Goodman, Howard 55
Gore, Albert 54
Governor and Mrs. Bob Graham 40, 44
Governor and Mrs. Edmund G. Brown 55
Governor Bob Graham 18
Governor Lawton Chiles 77
Governor's Club 20

gowns 88
Gracida, Memo 44
Graham, Governor and Mrs. Bob 15
Graham, Katherine 76
Grant, Cary 9
Grettenberger, John O. 44
Griffin, Merv 9, 44
Grinberg, Jerry 44
Gubelmann, Barton and Walter 5, 46

H

Hailand, Arthur 40
hairdressers 101
Hammer Art Collection 67
Hammer, Dr. Armand
    2, 11, 29, 44, 55, 66
Hammer v. Hammer 66
Hammer-Roberts letters 62
handbags 114, 116
handshaking 31
Harrods 84, 97, 100
Harrods department store 94
haute couture 53
Hawkins, Paula 54
HEALTH AND WEALTH, PALM BEACH
    STYLE 88, 106
Heinz, Dreu 79
Hewitt, Michael 21, 40
High Fashion 52
His Majesty the Sultan of Oman 54
Historical Society of Palm Beach County
    90
Hitler 5
Hogarth Etching 104
Hogarth, William 105
homeless 92, 110
Hoover, J. Edgar 12
Hope, Bob 9, 56
Hope, Bob and Dolores 51
House of Kahn 46
House of Windsor 4, 100

I

Ilyinsky, Paul 10, 11
"instant celebrities" 57, 59
Instrument of Abdication 8, 100
"International Queen of Hearts Dress Tour"
    89
internet 82
invitations 9, 13
Irish-American Unity Conference 45

J

Jacqueline Kennedy Onassis 104
jewels 6
Jewish Community 98
John, Elton 99
Judge Edward Rodgers 67
Judge James R. Knott 6

K

Kaye, Mort 56
Kelley, Kitty 94
Kensington couch potatoes 115
Kensington Palace 114
Kent, Geoffrey 74
key-to-the-city 21
King Charles I 20
King Constantine of Greece 75

King Edward VIII 5, 35, 38, 100
King George 36
King George VI 94
King Henry VIII 37, 94, 104
Klein, Milton 42
Kluge, John 75
Kluge, Pat 17, 19
Kremlin connection 12

L

land mines 92, 110
Last Duchess, The 8
Lauder, Estee and Joseph 5, 6
Lauren, Ralph 76
Leicaster Codex 67
Leidesdorf, Arthur 55
Leidesdorf, Tova 53
Lenin 11
Lennon, John 94
leprosy 110
Liberty Lobby 12
Light, Ann 46
limousines 20
Lord Mountbatten 2

M

Main Street News 111
"malice in the palace" 84, 109
Maltese Crosses 117
Manalapan 16
Mar-a-Lago 75, 87
Mar-a-Lago Club 82
Marix, Nigel 40, 42
Marks, Lana
    89, 92, 95, 96, 99, 111, 113
Mayor Carol Roberts
    13, 19, 20, 21, 22, 25, 41, 49, 69
Mayor "Deedy" Marix 40, 55
Memorial Service in Palm Beach 112
Miami 77
Miami Herald, The 3
Mills, Yvonne 46
Mitchell, Anita 115
Monroe, Marilyn 94
Mother Teresa 101

N

National Day of Recognition for the
    humanitarian 112
"New Age Princess" 94
Nixon, Richard 12, 49
Nizer, Louis 9, 54
Nobel Peace Prize 11, 67
Norton Gallery 23
Norton Gallery Exhibit 25
Norton Gallery Reception 27
NutraSweet® 104, 108

O

Occidental Petroleum Company 25
Onassis, Jacqueline Kennedy 100, 104
Order of St. George 116
Order of St. John Hospitaller 116
Outward Bound 78

P

Palm Beach 111
Palm Beach County Commissioner Carol A.
    Roberts 105

Palm Beach Daily News
    13, 15, 26, 32, 87, 112
Palm Beach Knights and Dames of Malta
    116
Palm Beach patients 30
Palm Beach Polo and Country Club
    43, 65, 79
Palm Beach Rotary Club 82
Papamarkou, Alexander 75
Paparazzi 93, 99, 103
Parliament 102
patient encounters 61
patients 108
Paul, Henri 104
Peck, Gregory 9, 25, 27, 54, 71
Penske, Roger 54
"People's Princess" 92
People's Princess Charitable Foundation 89
Permission for Charitable Solicitation 11
Perot, H. Ross 9, 27, 44, 54, 74
personal courage 110
personal diplomacy 20
"Personal Friend" 115
personal reflections 103
Petho, Ellen Louise 89
Phillips, Abigail Van Buren 54
photographers 41, 46
Pioneer Linens 46
plea for professional tolerance 109
polo 43, 64
polo match 23
Port Diana 101
Post, Marjorie Merriweather 5, 10, 16, 46
postage stamps 90
"POW" 95
preparations 20
Preservation Foundation of Palm Beach 11
President and Mrs. John F. Kennedy 69
President Bill Clinton 70
President John F. Kennedy 41
President Reagan 41
Presley, Elvis 94
press, the 18
Prime Minister Margaret Thatcher 106
Prime Minister Menachem Begin 67
Prince Charles
    3, 4, 8, 29, 36, 44, 56, 74, 83, 102
Prince Edward 35, 78, 79
Prince Harry 98
Prince Michael de Bourbon-Parme 79
Prince Michael of Yugoslavia 54, 79
Prince of Wales 2, 65
Prince of Yugoslavia 27
Prince Philip 78
Prince William 116
Princess Anne 79
Princess Diana 3, 37, 52, 76, 83, 85, 87
Princess Diana Bride Dolls 101
Princess Diana Memorial Trust Fund 100
Princess Diana of Wales Street 101
Princess Grace of Monaco 93, 94
Princess Margaret 78
Princess Maria Pia de Savoye 79
Princess of Wales 96
Problems of a Royal Family 81
Protocol: The Complete Handbook of
    Diplomatic, Official and Social
    Usage 32

Pulitzer, Herbert 5
Pulitzer, Roxanne 16

Q

quasi-royalty 106
Queen Elizabeth II
    4, 36, 76, 84, 94, 95, 102, 116
Queen Mother 96
Queen of Hearts 37
Queen of Style 88
Queen Sirikit 10
Queen Victoria 4
quick-change artist 106

R

Rabbi Chaim Wender 99
Reverend John Mangrum 18, 43
Reverend Ralph R. Warren, Jr. 112
Rhodes, Zandra 89
Ritz Hotel of Paris 97
Roberts Angels 109
Roberts, Carol 65, 75, 107, 108, 115
Roberts, Dr. H.J. 40
Rockefeller, Laurance S. 54
Rolls Royce 34, 75, 77
Roosevelt, Eleanor 46
Rorech, Maureen 89
Ross, Diana 3
royal adultery 81
Royal Couple 29
royal enigmas 81
royal history 3
royal indifference/neglect 96
royal manners 31
Royal Marriages Act 81
"royal scam" 86
royal trivia 28, 35
Royal Wedding 4

S

Sachs, Rose 53, 55
Sanford, Mary 16, 90
Sansbury, John 40
Scaasi, Arnold 90
Schmidlapp, Pat 46
Schwarzenegger, Arnold 104
Scooter in Palm Beach 65, 107, 108
Scripp, Betty 90
seat belt 104
security 40, 50, 104
self-esteem 95
Senator Lawton Chiles 49
Senator Paula Hawkins 9
sense of humor 95
separation 83
sexually abused 110
Simpson, Wallis Warfield 5, 8
"Single Mother" 95
Sloane Rangers 4
Smith, E.T. 10
societal revenge 16
Sotheby's 6, 8, 100
Soviet Premier Konstantin Chernenko 11
Spencer, Charles 104
Spencer, Robert 113
Spencers 37, 98
Stallone, Sylvester 94
Statute of Westminster 35
Street, Main News 112
superstar model 38

T

table etiquette 32
Tankoos, Ruth and Joe 5
terminally-ill 110
Thayer, Dodie 77
The Ball 11, 54
"the common language" 37
The Evening Times 15, 19, 27
"the fine print of fame" 94
"the first wives club" 85
"the frenzy of renown" 94
the media 13
The Miami Herald 19
"the most photographed woman in the
    world" 92, 95, 101
The Palm Beach Post 18
"The Palm Beach Princess" 101
"The People's Princess" 96, 110
"the pose" 46
The Prince of Wales 83
"the princess inside every woman" 96
The Royal Marriages 83
"the silent princess" 84
The Spencers 94
The Will to Help 110
thoughts of suicide 96
threatened monarchy 102
tiaras 32, 37, 46
ticket prices 10
titles 3, 31, 33
"touch of royalty" 108
Town Council 10
trauma care 105
Travolta, John 89, 95
Trump, Donald 54, 57, 75, 102
Tuchbreiter, Helene 16
Turner, Ted 9, 27, 44, 54
tuxedo encounter 59
twelve good rules 32

U

U.S. Constitution 3
Union Jack 35
United World College of the American West
    2, 11, 56
United World Colleges 2

V

vegetarianism 36
Viking Princess 72
Viscountess Mary Rothermere 79
Vizcaya 77

W

Wainscott, Barbara 78, 80
Walker, Catherine 89
Walton, Sam 68
Warfield, S. Davies 6
warped psychologic inferences 110
Washington, George 37, 98
Weier, Robin 46
Weintraub, Jerry 54
Wellington 18
WEST PALM BEACH: CENTENNIAL
    REFLECTIONS 10, 113, 116
Westminster Abbey 98
Whitney, Marylou Vanderbilt
    46, 53, 55, 75, 90
Widener, Lewis 9

Wiggins, Ron 44
William Kennedy Smith rape trial 104
William the Conqueror 76
Williamsburg, Virginia 76
Wilmot, Mollie 16
Windsor Castle 5
wines 55
Woldridge, Jane 36
Worldwide Fund for Nature 78
Wright, Sir Oliver 54

Y

Ylvisaker, Jane 53
Ylvisaker, William 44, 65
Young, Robert 5
Your Worship 106

Z

Zsa Zsa Gabor 64